Men of
Brave Heart

Men of
Brave Heart

The Virtue
of Courage
in the
Priestly Life

The Most Rev. José H. Gomez, S.T.D.
Archbishop of San Antonio

Our Sunday Visitor Publishing Division
Our Sunday Visitor, Inc.
Huntington, Indiana 46750

Nihil Obstat:
Rev. Michael Heintz, Ph.D.
Censor Librorum

Imprimatur:
✠ John M. D'Arcy
Bishop of Fort Wayne-South Bend
May 14, 2009

The *Nihil Obstat* and *Imprimatur* are official declarations that a book is free from doctrinal or moral error. It is not implied that those who have granted the *Nihil Obstat* and *Imprimatur* agree with the contents, opinions, or statements expressed.

Interior design by Sherri L. Hoffman
Cover design by Amanda Miller
Cover photo by Al Rendon, courtesy of the Archdiocese of San Antonio

PRINTED IN THE UNITED STATES OF AMERICA

Contents

PREFACE

THIS IS A BOOK FOR priests. I have thought for many years about what a mystery it is that God calls ordinary men to share in his plan for the salvation of the world. The priest alone is configured to Christ so that he stands in the person of the Savior himself, a messenger and vessel of the mercy of God. Yet at the same time, the priest remains a man like others, not noticeably different on the outside from the rest of the men.

What distinguishes the priest is always his heart. The priest has a special heart — the heart of a disciple and a missionary; a heart that longs to share the joy of Jesus Christ with his brothers and sisters. Men do not come to the priesthood because they have calculated that it will be a good professional move. They do not come for the money or even the opportunity to do useful and interesting work. They come because they are compelled to come, because they have heard a call. Like Abraham and Mary. Like James and John and all the Twelve. "Do you love me more than these?" Jesus asked Peter. With Peter and the apostles, the priest has said, "Yes, Lord. You know that I love you."

To heed such a call, a call that comes personally from the living God, a man needs a generous heart. To live out that call over the course of a lifetime, to give himself totally to God, a man needs a brave heart. Nothing human is alien to the priest. He sees it all. Every parish is a microcosm, a miniature world in which countless human dramas and dreams play out. The priest walks with his people as they are born and as they die; he is with them in times of joy and times of sorrow; in sickness and suffering, in health and happiness.

It was said of Jesus that "he himself knew what was in man" (John 2:25). This is true of his priests, too. The priest knows what is in man — he knows the depths that people can sink to, and the glorious heights they can climb to by the grace of God. He hears their confessions, and heals them of their sins. He feeds their deepest hungers with the Bread of Life. He preaches the Word of God in a world that has nearly forgotten him.

I am surprised by the humility of most priests. They are men of virtue, prayer, learning, and deep love, and yet so often they will admit feeling inadequate to the tasks they have been given, saying they do not feel wise enough or holy enough. On one level they are right, of course. Who could be worthy of such a calling, to be an ambassador and a steward of the mysteries of God? And yet each one knows that he has been called by name, chosen by God himself. Each one can say what St. Paul said: "By the grace of God, I am what I am" (1 Cor. 15:9–10).

I wrote this book to encourage priests to persevere in that grace, in the great mission that God has given them. You need a brave heart to be a priest — especially to be a priest called to the new evangelization of the Americas. How do we lead men and women to God in a culture where so many have lost their way and live as if he no longer exists? It takes courage, or what the Catholic tradition calls "fortitude," one of the four cardinal virtues. But courage is not something we are born with. It is a virtue that must be accepted, learned, and cultivated.

My hope is that this book will assist priests in their lifelong growth in virtue and holiness. The book itself grows out of my doctoral studies in the Christian anthropology and moral philosophy of St. Thomas Aquinas. But this is not an academic book. What I hope to do is present the fruits of serious, prayerful study — of the Scriptures, of St. Thomas and the Church Fathers, of the writings of today's best moral theologians

— and bring it all to bear on the pastoral task of priestly formation. What is especially important to me is the witness of the Church's saints and martyrs, especially priests and deacons. The lives of the saints are "lived theology." In them we see the word of the Church's theology and teaching made flesh.

I know from my own experience the life-changing influence a good priest can have on a person's life. There was a very holy priest who used to celebrate the early morning Mass at the local parish during my college years in Mexico City. Every day Padre Gaspar would begin to cry during the consecration, because he was aware of the incredible miracle that was happening on the altar at his hands.

In 1970, when I was still a teenager, I met another priest, a visitor from Spain, who was obviously a man of prayer and virtue, with a deep love for Jesus Christ. Those were challenging and confusing times, with many changes going on inside the Church and in society. Many were questioning the Church's teachings and its relevance in the modern world. In the midst of all this, this priest had a peacefulness and calm about him. Yet he was also insistent about the truth of the Gospel and the urgency of evangelization. The unconditional fidelity of this faithful priest was striking, and his optimism about the future of the Church was contagious.

This encounter changed the direction of my life. Looking back on it, I have no doubt that the witness of that saintly priest was instrumental in my own discernment of my vocation. It took great courage to speak and live the way he did, and I have never forgotten his priestly example. Many years later I had the privilege of being in St. Peter's Square in Rome when he was canonized as St. Josemaría Escrivá de Balaguer.

I have known many holy priests whose names will probably never be written in the history books or in the rolls of the saints. But they were saints nonetheless even if the fruits of their ministries are known only to God and to the people whose lives they touched.

One of these priests was Father John O'Shea, who was assigned to the cathedral in Denver when I was serving as auxiliary bishop there. A late vocation to the priesthood, Father O'Shea was a former deputy police chief, a widower, and a father of ten children. He suffered a heart attack two days after his ordination at the age of 69. While he was recovering, doctors discovered that he had a brain tumor. Within four months he was dead. But he left me with a wonderful example of courage and trust in God's will. He was a joyful man, even in his sickness. One day, as he was coming out of the sacristy, I asked him how he was doing. He said, "I am the happiest person in the world because I just said Mass."

As I was finishing this book, the Holy Father, Pope Benedict XVI, announced the convocation of a special "Year for Priests," to mark the 150th anniversary of the death of the patron saint of priests, St. John Vianney. So I offer this book as a humble contribution to the Pope's initiative, which seeks to call attention to the missionary vocation of the priest in the world of the third millennium. St. John Vianney once said: "The priesthood is the love of the heart of Jesus." I pray that this book can aide in the growth and formation of the priestly heart — which is always the heart of a disciple, the heart of a missionary, and the heart of Christ.

I write as a bishop, but always too as a "priest forever." I have been ordained now for more than thirty years, and my priesthood is the profound joy and privilege of my life. I can think of no more beautiful way to spend one's life than to spend it in the priestly service of our Lord. And I thank God for this gift every day.

I dedicate this book to my brother priests in San Antonio, Texas, my first collaborators in the mission of the new evangelization. In a special way I dedicate this work also to all seminarians — past, present, and future — of Assumption Seminary in San Antonio. St. Rafael Guízar Valencia, the missionary saint of Mexico, said: "A bishop can do without the miter, the crozier, and even without the cathedral. But he cannot do without the seminary, since the future of his diocese depends on it." Every bishop knows this, and I am grateful beyond words to all who open their hearts in love to the priestly calling of Jesus Christ.

I pray that this work in some way will help all priests and seminarians to draw near in confidence to the throne of grace (Heb. 4:16). And I entrust everything to the tender intercession of the Mother of Priests, Our Lady of Guadalupe.

The Most Rev. José H. Gomez, S.T.D.
Archbishop of San Antonio, Texas
March 25, 2009
Solemnity of the Annunciation of Our Lord

CHAPTER 1

The Beginning of Strong Courage

The Virtues, the Priesthood, and the
New Evangelization of America

FATHER ANTONIO MARGIL, A FRANCISCAN, is one of many nearly forgotten priest-heroes of America's first evangelization. He was ordained in Spain at the age of 24, and left his home forever in 1683. He set sail for the New World because there, as he told his mother, "millions of souls are lost for want of priests to dispel the darkness of unbelief."[1]

For the next 43 years, Father Antonio roamed all over this continent, covering thousands of miles of uncharted territory. He walked barefoot and took with him only a walking stick, his breviary, and a small kit for saying Mass. He would travel forty or fifty miles a day this way. People called him "the Flying Padre." He established churches in Costa Rica, Nicaragua, Guatemala, Mexico, Panama, Louisiana, and Texas. Through his priestly ministry, the darkness of unbelief was dispelled and millions of souls came to know the life-changing encounter with Jesus Christ and his Gospel.

Father Antonio's days were long, lonely, and filled with toil. Often he preached to large crowds in the evening, sometimes until past midnight; he rose early and spent the daytime hours teaching catechism, baptizing, hearing confessions, celebrating Mass, and supervising social and charitable works. He fasted and performed other penances for the sake of the souls he sought to win.

Often on his missionary sojourns he faced hostile bands of natives, and many times he just barely escaped death. Near the Guazamota River in Mexico his missionary party was confronted by Nayarits tribesmen brandishing machetes. Another time he was almost burned at the stake. Another time still, he was tied to a tree and threatened by a firing squad of a dozen men armed with bows and arrows.

Yet his experiences are not unique. The missionary history of the Americas is filled with these kind of stories. I am thinking of the fruitful and heroic work of men like St. Isaac Jogues and St. John de Brébeuf and their priestly companions; St. Juan Macias; St. Roque González; the Franciscan missionaries martyred in what is now Georgia in 1597. The list could go on for pages. The seeds of the Gospel were sown in the New World with the blood of many priest-martyrs and the anonymous sweat and sacrifice of countless more.

What enabled these priests to endure thankless drudgery and hardships for years on end, to risk their lives to preach to and sacrifice for people — many of whom hated them and wished them dead? Certainly, these pioneers of the faith in America were motivated by their love for Jesus Christ and their belief that all people must hear his Gospel and "receive our holy Catholic faith for their eternal salvation." That is how Father Eusebio Kino, the great Jesuit missionary of Arizona, put it in 1710.[2]

But the question remains: what sustained these priests' zeal in times of tedium, trial, or dejection? How did they avoid burning-out or keeping their ministries from becoming merely the performance of required duties? I believe it was their practice of *the virtues*, and in a special way, the virtue of *fortitude*, also known as *courage*. The missionary priests of America's first evangelization were men trained and formed in such a way that they habitually exercised the three "theological" virtues of *faith, hope,* and *love* as well as the four "moral" virtues of *prudence, temperance, justice,* and *fortitude.*

Since the early days of the Church, these seven virtues have been understood as the "excellences" characteristic of the true disciple of Christ. Although unfortunately they are not enough known or taught today, the virtues remain the true measure of the Christian personality. The Church's canonized saints are defined as those who practice the virtues to a "heroic" degree, cooperating with God's grace.[3] And as St. Paul often reminded the first Christians, all baptized believers are "called to be saints."[4] In other words, every Christian is called to lead a life animated by the virtues.

Paul described this virtuous life near the end of his letter to the Philippians:

> Whatever is true, whatever is honorable, whatever is just, whatever is pure, whatever is lovely, whatever is gracious, if there is any excellence, if there is anything worthy of praise, think about these things.[5]

Paul's catalogue of the virtues here reflects the influence of classical Greek and Roman philosophy. The Catholic tradition of the virtues grew out of the early encounter of Jewish and Christian thought with the surrounding Hellenistic culture. This encounter is attested to not only in St. Paul and elsewhere in the New Testament; it can be seen even earlier — in the Greek canon of Jewish Scriptures known as the Septuagint.

In the book of Wisdom, which was written in Greek and came out of the Jewish community in Alexandria, Egypt, about a hundred years before Christ, we read that the work of divine Wisdom is to produce the virtues in those who love her:

> Her labors are virtues; for she teaches self-control and prudence, justice and courage; nothing in life is more profitable for men than these.[6]

Here we see the beginnings of the biblical transformation of the four virtues of classical Hellenistic philosophy. For the Greeks and Romans, the virtues (*aretē* or "excellence" in Greek; *virtus*, "power" or "manliness" in Latin) were part of the response to one of philosophy's basic questions — how should men and women live? This questioning is heard in the dialogues of Plato and is taken up in a more systematic way in the writings of Aristotle. For Aristotle, men and women achieve happiness (*eudaimonia*), which is the goal of their existence, by possessing and exercising the virtues.

By the time of Jesus, the four-fold division of the virtues (prudence, temperance, justice, and fortitude) was presumed in Hellenistic thought on morals, ethics, and character development. Writing about 45 years before Christ, the Roman statesman and philosopher Cicero proposed: "Each man should so conduct himself that *fortitude* appears in labors and dangers; *temperance* in foregoing pleasures; *prudence* in the choice between good and evil; *justice* in giving every man his own."[7]

Adapted in the Christian tradition, these became known as the "cardinal virtues" (from the Latin *cardo,* "hinge"). It is thought that the first to characterize the virtues this way may have been St. Ambrose, the bishop of Milan. In his book, *On the Duties of the Clergy,* written in 391, Ambrose concludes a discussion of the Old Testament patriarchs:

> What duty connected with the chief virtues was wanting in these men? In the first place they showed *prudence,* which is exercised in the search of the truth, and which imparts a desire for full knowledge; next, *justice,* which assigns each man his own, does not claim another's, and disregards its own advantage, so as to guard the rights of all; thirdly, *fortitude,* which both in warfare and at home is conspicuous in greatness of mind and distinguishes itself in the strength of the body; fourthly, *temperance,*

which preserves the right method and order in all things that we think should either be done or said.[8]

Today, we might best think of the cardinal virtues as the four hinges of the narrow gate that Christ spoke of, the gate that opens us to eternal life.[9] The virtues are those excellences that make us truly human, that make it possible for us to fully become the people that God intends us to be. As the twentieth-century Catholic philosopher, Joseph Pieper, has written: "Virtue is the utmost of what a man can be; it is the realization of the human capacity for being."[10] In his important essay, "On the Rehabilitation of Virtue" (1913), Catholic philosopher Max Scheler said the *halo* is a perfect symbol of what we mean by the virtues.

> The Christian symbol of the halo let virtue shine spontaneously from the depths of the person and made visible the idea that the goodness and beauty of virtue ... rests primarily in the high and noble nature of the being and essence of the soul.[11]

Jesus Christ, the Virtue of God

The traditional Christian conception of the virtues owes a lot to the formulations of Hellenistic philosophy and culture. But in the writings of the Church Fathers we see important adaptations and modifications. We get the strong sense that the classical virtues were somehow incomplete, that they were waiting for their necessary and ultimate fulfillment in the teaching of Christ.

The Fathers, following the authors of sacred Scripture, taught that Jesus was the divine Wisdom and *Logos*, and hence the true source and teacher of the virtues. Ambrose wrote: "He is the beginning of all things, and the Author of each several virtue.... From him each several virtue has taken its origin."[12]

Origen, writing in the late second century, had the same idea: "Do not be surprised that we speak of the virtues loving Christ, since in other cases we are wont to regard Christ as himself the substance of those very virtues."[13]

The Fathers here were following the teaching of the New Testament. The Latin translation of 1 Corinthians 1:24 speaks of *Christum Dei virtutem et Dei sapientiam* ("Christ, the virtue of God and the wisdom of God"). The Christian idea of the virtues came to be associated with the broader Christian understanding of the nature and destiny of the human person. In Jesus — who is true God and true man, the image of the invisible God and the new Adam — humanity discovers the true meaning of its creation "in the image and likeness of God."[14]

Christ is the man of perfect virtue, the embodiment and model of every virtue. In his person and teaching we see the human virtues transfigured. In our new life in Christ, which begins in baptism, God "infuses" us with the virtues — pouring them into us by the power of the Holy Spirit, giving us the qualities and dispositions we need to live in his image as children of God. Christian theologians came to call the virtues of the Greeks and Romans the *acquired* or *natural virtues*. The theologians understood, as the philosophers did, that by our natural powers we can acquire the good habits of prudence, justice, fortitude, and temperance. We can learn the virtues and put them into practice in our own lives, and we can grow in these virtues through our repetition of virtuous thoughts, habits, and actions. The natural virtues we acquire can make us "good pagans" — that is, men and women who are good citizens, good parents, good friends and neighbors.

But Christ taught that we are made for far more than natural goodness. We are made for divine filiation — to be children of God. The virtues we need to lead that kind of life cannot be acquired by our own powers. It is simply not possible for us to merit or achieve the virtues necessary for such an elevated, supernatural kind of life. In fact, because of the wounds inflicted on our nature by original sin, it is difficult for us to even maintain the "moral balance" necessary to lead a life of natural virtue.[15]

That said, we still need to strive to acquire and practice the natural virtues in order to be good and to lay the natural groundwork upon which God's grace can build. And God gives us his grace in baptism, making us children of God and partakers of the divine nature.[16] Along with the grace of divine sonship that sanctifies us, he gives us virtues and spiritual gifts to make us worthy of that inheritance. The theological virtues of faith, hope, and love are poured into our hearts and abide with us.[17] He also infuses us with the moral virtues we need to fully partake of the divine nature and to grow in goodness.[18] In addition, he gives us seven gifts of the Holy Spirit that assist us until the virtues abound in us and we reach full maturity in Christ.[19]

This is a key difference between the Christian and the classical Greek and Roman understanding of the virtues. The Christian believes that the human person lives a new life by the Spirit of God, that Christ has bestowed on us the virtues as divine powers that enable us to love and serve him as his children. St. Augustine said: "Virtue is a good quality of the mind, by which one lives righteously, of which no one can make bad use, which God works in us without us."[20]

Each part of that definition is important. First, virtue is a quality of the mind; that is, it is an interior principle of heart and soul. The virtues are infused in us and become a part of our being. As a divine principle within us, the virtues cannot be misused; they are there to lead us to righteousness. Virtue is the work of God who infuses the virtues in us wholly apart from our own merits or powers.

By the infused virtues we are able to develop and exercise those capacities of the soul by which we can live and work — not in servile obedience to divine commands, not out of fear of punishment — but with the love and gratitude of sons and daughters.[21]

The infused virtue of *faith* makes us aware of the reality of God and enables us to *hope* in the promises of divine revelation, especially the promise of our resurrection. Through the virtue of *charity* we are able to direct all our thoughts and actions to attaining the "end" or goal of our faith and hope — namely, union with God in communion with our neighbors. The infused moral virtues of prudence, justice, fortitude, and temperance provide us with the means for achieving that end.

In the light of Jesus and his Gospel, the traditional moral or cardinal virtues are seen in a new, supernatural dimension.

Prudence (Greek: *phronēsis*; Latin: *prudentia*) is the divine gift that enables a man to seek the truth and the good in every circumstance, and to desire always the right means to attain these things. The prudent man builds the house of his life, not upon the shifting sands of his own desires and appetites, but upon the solid rock of Christ's words and teachings.

Justice (*dikaiosyne; jus*) is the virtue that causes us to seek the Kingdom of God and his righteousness before all else. The just man hungers and thirsts for God's will to be done on earth as it is in heaven, working for a world in which men and women treat one another as they would like to be treated, with mercy and compassion.

Temperance (*sōphrosynē; temperantia*) is the virtue by which we train ourselves to control our appetites and passions. The temperate man is not anxious for what he might eat or drink, but does all things, even eating and drinking, for the glory of God.

Finally, fortitude (*andreia; fortitūdō*) is the willingness to suffer persecution and even death for the sake of Christ and the truth of his Gospel. The courageous man denies himself and takes up his cross, knowing that Christ has conquered the world.

In addition to the seven infused virtues, God gives us seven gifts of his Spirit — *wisdom, understanding, counsel, fortitude, knowledge, piety,* and *fear of the Lord* — to complete and perfect those virtues in us. The seven gifts, which are possessed fully by Christ, are intended to lead us to blessedness and communion with God, by inspiring us to ever closer imitation of him.[22]

We can see why the Fathers of the Church wrote in such soaring language about the beauty of the virtues in the Christian life. St. Gregory, a third-century bishop known as the "Wonderworker," wrote that the virtues were God's artwork in the believer's soul: "The virtues are very great and lofty, and can only be attained by someone in whom God has breathed his power.... And the end of everything I consider to be nothing but this: that by a pure mind we make ourselves like God, that we may draw near to him and abide in him."[23]

The Christian understands the virtues not as a series of rules or commandments to be followed. Nor are they a set of skills to be learned or obtained. The goal of the virtuous life is to become like God himself through an imitation of Christ and a sharing in the blessedness of the divine life through the gifts of his Spirit and grace.

The Virtuous Life and the Imitation of God

"The end of the life of virtue is to be like God," St. Gregory of Nyssa says in his first sermon on the Beatitudes.[24] The goal of the infused virtues, which are given to us by the grace of God, is to lead us to the contemplation of Virtue himself — Jesus Christ. In this passage from Augustine, we hear an echo of a teaching that originates in St. Paul — that through our contemplation of Christ and our imitation of his virtues we are to be changed into his likeness.[25]

> From these virtues we go on to *a virtue*. To what virtue? To "Christ, the Virtue of God and the Wisdom of God" (1 Cor. 1:24).... [F]or all the virtues that are necessary and useful in this valley of weeping shall yield one virtue, himself. In Scripture and in many writers, four virtues are described as useful for life: *prudence,* by which we discern between good and evil; *justice,* by which we give each person his due, "owing no man anything" but loving all men (Rom. 13:8); *temperance,* by which we restrain lusts; and *fortitude,* by which we bear all troubles.
>
> These virtues are now, by the grace of God, given unto us in this valley of weeping. From these virtues we mount unto the other virtue. And what will that be, but the virtue of the contemplation of God alone?... "They shall go from virtue to virtue." What virtue? That of contemplation. What is contemplation? "The God of gods shall appear in Zion." The God of gods, Christ of the Christians.... He shall appear to the pure of heart.[26]

In our day, it is urgent that we recover this beautiful and exciting vision of the early Church — this sense of the Christian life as an adventure in holiness, a journey to the Father who calls us in love; a daily walking in intimacy with Jesus as a child of God, imitating his virtues and striving in grace to scale the heights of virtue, fulfilling the commandment of Christ: "You, therefore, must be perfect, as your heavenly Father is perfect."[27] As Paul wrote to the Thessalonians: "For this is the will of God — your sanctification."[28]

Since the Second Vatican Council, this will of God has been identified as "the universal call to holiness."[29] However, we seem to have lost sight of the essential connection between holiness and the virtues. Few people today seem to recognize that the virtues are "constitutive elements of Christian holiness," as the Dominican spiritual theologian, Father Jordan Aumann, has termed it.[30]

The universal call to holiness presumes the virtues as the essential "content" of holiness. Holiness is the perfection of charity, the perfection of the love of God and neighbor in imitation of Christ and with the help of his grace. But without an understanding of the virtues, the notion of charity, and hence the notion of holiness, will remain vague or shapeless.

The virtues are means, not ends. They exist to further our efforts to fulfill Christ's new commandment of love.[31] The Christian life flows from the theological virtues of faith, hope, and charity.[32] In turn, charity is "the form of the virtues," as the *Catechism* says. "By charity, we love God above all things and our neighbor as ourselves for love of God. Charity, the form of all the virtues, 'binds everything together in perfect harmony' (Col. 3:14)."[33]

This is the ancient teaching of the Church. Augustine said the virtues are nothing more than "four forms of love," four aspects of the love of God.

> I hold virtue to be nothing else than perfect love of God … the chief good, the highest wisdom, the perfect harmony…. [T]*emperance* is love keeping itself entire and incorrupt for God; *fortitude* is love bearing everything readily for the sake of God; *justice* is love serving God only, and therefore ruling well all else, as subject to man; *prudence* is love making a right distinction between what helps it towards God and what might hinder it.[34]

A holy person is one who loves God and neighbor perfectly, expressing that love in the practice of the virtues. St. Francis de Sales speaks for the whole tradition when he describes charity as the "queen of all virtues."[35] In his beautiful notion, our love of God is the motive principle that underlies our cooperation with grace and our growth in the virtues: "If the love in a heart is zealous, powerful, and excellent, it will also enrich and perfect the works of the virtues that proceed from it."[36]

In our practice of the virtues we become beloved children of our Father, "imitators of God" who is love.[37] The call to holiness is the call to a virtuous life, a divinized life, a life like God's. St. Thomas Aquinas makes a profound summary of the Christian vision: "Virtue consists in the following, or imitation, of God."[38]

The Loss of Virtue

It is unfortunate that we have lost our appreciation for the virtues and their place in the spiritual and moral life. The reasons for this situation are complicated and remain the subject of debate by fine scholars in a number of disciplines.[39] Getting into the details of this debate is beyond my purposes here. What can be said simply and briefly is that Western culture has lost its capacity to think and talk about virtue and goodness.

Our intellectual culture is increasingly skeptical that there can be such things as objective truths or moral absolutes such as "the good," "the right," or "the beautiful." Seldom do we see in our arts or popular media portrayals of goodness. Instead a doubtful gaze is cast on the possible self-interest or hidden motives that might be behind any act of seeming goodness. We are always wondering: "What was in it for them?"

The ancient belief that truths and moral absolutes exist and can be known by reason as well as by faith has given way to an extreme relativism or, at best, a subjectivist or utilitarian ethic.[40] Simply put, we no longer believe there are truths, we think there are only opinions. Actions are neither "right" nor "wrong"; instead, they are to be judged according to their relative utility or success in fulfilling one's own desires or attaining one's own goals.

In such a culture, the idea of virtue and character formation makes no sense. In addition, we have seen the rise of a counterfeit idea of freedom in our culture — freedom defined as radical autonomy, and the ability to be liberated from every standard of virtue that comes from outside the individual. Freedom today is no longer the freedom to choose excellence and virtue, it is rather the "freedom of indifference."[41]

At the same time, it is true that in the Church we have not yet fully appropriated the fruits of the renewal in moral theology heralded by Pope John Paul II's encyclical *Veritatis Splendor* and the *Catechism of the Catholic Church*. Our thinking about Christian character development still bears the stamp of the older tradition of the moral manuals.

This tradition, as Pope Benedict XVI has acknowledged, arose from the practical need to provide priests with "concrete answers to the questions that might arise in the context of confession." But as a consequence, the Church's beautiful vision was abbreviated into a legalistic, pragmatic emphasis on precepts, duties, and rules of conduct. What was lost, as the Pope has said, was the sense of the Christian life as "a living encounter with a living person who is Christ" — an encounter that "stirs up love," from which "everything else flows."[42]

The Renewal of Priestly Identity

We face a crisis of virtue. By that I mean that the virtues have little or no meaning in the lives of ordinary believers or in the lives of many priests. We need to recover the sense of the Christian life as the response of the soul to the love of God in Christ, a response expressed in the thirst for holiness and the practice of the virtues. If this is true for everyone in the Church today, it is an especially urgent priority for priests.

"A great dignity," St. Lawrence Justinian exclaimed in speaking of the priesthood. "But great, too, is the responsibility. Placed high in the eyes of men, they must also be lifted up to the peak of virtue before the eye of him who sees all."[43] This is the ancient and constant teaching of the Church's saints and doctors. The priest stands before the Church as the image of Christ, who is the Virtue of God and the man of virtue *par excellence*. For the great mission entrusted to the priest by the sacrament of Holy Orders, "ordinary goodness does not suffice, but superior virtue is required," as Thomas Aquinas said.[44]

Now, it is important that we make sure we are clear here on a couple of points. The priest or the seminarian is not expected to be a perfect man, a man without sin. The priest or seminarian, like every other Christian, is a person on a spiritual journey of daily repentence and conversion. Christ said he came not to call the righteous, but sinners. And as St. Paul said, quoting the prophets, "None is righteous, no, not one."[45]

The universal call to holiness is the call that Christ makes to sinners — to all of us, clergy, religious, and laity alike — to repent and believe in the Gospel. Christ did not imagine a one-time conversion. Every Christian life, even the life of the priest, is a life of daily conversion. It is a lifelong process by which we try daily to more and more conform our lives to Christ and to his teaching.

This is the context in which we must understand the special responsibility of the priestly vocation. The priest is a Christian like all others in his need for conversion in imitation of Christ. But because of his special closeness to Christ, he is also called to be a model of holiness for the souls under his care. He must be able say with St. Paul: "Be imitators of me, as I am of Christ."[46] In his encyclical on the priesthood, *Ad Catholici Sacerdotii*, Pope Pius XI explained this principle in words that are inspiring and still timely:

The priest must teach the truths of faith. But the truths of religion are never so worthily and effectively taught as when taught by virtue, because in the common saying: "Deeds speak louder than words."... St. Gregory the Great gives the reason: "The voice which penetrates the hearts of the hearers, is the voice commended by the speaker's own life; because what his word enjoins, his example helps to bring about."[47]

Again, it is important for the priest to remember that he is not called to superhuman perfection. But, as the Code of Canon Law stipulates: "In leading their lives, clerics are bound in a special way to pursue holiness since, having been consecrated to God by a new title in the reception of Orders, they are dispensers of the mysteries of God in the service of his people."[48]

The priest is called to lead and to serve. He does that by practicing the virtues and thereby providing inspiration and an example to his people in their own practice of the virtues. In the tradition of priestly formation, the imitation of Christ is at the heart of priestly spirituality, and so is the practice of the virtues. In the Liturgy of the Hours, the Church proposes that priests reflect upon this advice from St. Paul of the Cross:

It is very good and holy to consider the passion of our Lord and to meditate on it, for by this sacred path we reach union with God.... Be constant in practicing every virtue, and especially in imitating the patience of our dear Jesus, for this is the summit of pure love. Live in such a way that all may know that you bear outwardly as well as inwardly the image of Christ crucified. For if a man is united inwardly with the Son of the living God, he also bears his likeness outwardly by his continual practice of heroic goodness, and especially through a patience reinforced by courage, which does not complain either secretly or in public.[49]

In traditional works of spiritual direction and ascetical theology, the virtues play a pivotal role in priestly spirituality and identity.[50] However, it must be admitted that in the years following the Second Vatican Council, this theme was not talked about much — not only in spiritual theology but also in magisterial documents. In fact, the Council's two documents on the priesthood, *Presbyterorum Ordinis* and *Optatum Totius*, made no mention of the cardinal or moral virtues, although the former included a beautiful meditation on "the vocation of priests to the life of perfection," and the latter encouraged strengthening seminarians in "faith, hope, and charity" and teaching them to "obtain an increase of other virtues."[51] In general, however, it can seem as if the Council presumed the training in the virtues. But I do not think we can take such training for granted anymore.

Beginning with Pope John Paul and his apostolic exhortation *Pastores Dabo Vobis* (1992), we have seen a revived sense of the importance of the virtues.[52] The fifth edition of the United States Catholic bishops' *Program of Priestly Formation* (2006) rightly stresses the vital necessity of character development centered on the cardinal virtues. The man who would be a priest, the bishops say, must be "a man *who demonstrates the human virtues of prudence, fortitude, temperance, justice,* humility, constancy, sincerity, patience, good manners, truthfulness, and keeping his word, *and who also manifests growth in the practice of these virtues.*"[53]

The Vatican's Congregation for Catholic Education, in a 2008 document, also wisely counsels that the candidate for the priesthood must be helped in "acquiring those moral and theological virtues which are necessary for living, in coherence and interior freedom, the total gift of his life, so as to be a 'servant of the Church as communion.'"[54] It is significant, too, that during his first pastoral visit to the United States, Pope Benedict identified growth in the virtues as essential to priestly renewal and the Church's mission of evangelization.

> Indeed a clearer focus upon the imitation of Christ in holiness of life is exactly what is needed in order for us to move forward. We need to rediscover the joy of living a Christ-centered life, cultivating the virtues, and immersing ourselves in prayer.[55]

In the Pope's words we see a proper spiritual balance for the priest and men training for the priesthood. The priest or candidate is never presumed to be "already there." He is on a spiritual journey that involves a daily striving to imitate the holiness of Christ in joy, focused on Christ, and filled with prayer and the desire to grow in virtue.

Priests Must Have the Heart of Missionaries

The need for cultivating the virtues is especially important given the leadership expected of priests in the new evangelization. Priests are at the vanguard of the essential mission of the Church in the twenty-first century. As Pope John Paul said in his pastoral program for the Americas in the new millenium, this mission represents "a commitment, not to a re-evangelization, but to a new evangelization — new in ardor, methods, and expression."[56]

This new mission to America calls for priests who are men of prayer and Christ-like generosity and love. The priest is to lead by word and example as the Church seeks creative new ways to present the Gospel and the Catholic vision of reality to a culture that is pervasively secularized and materialistic and characterized by an extreme individualism and a radical pluralism of options for personal and spiritual fulfillment. By his witness and example, as much as by his formal ministry, the priest must call the men and women of our day to conversion — to that encounter with Jesus Christ through which they can be saved.

The demands of the new evangelization remind us that priestly identity is always missionary. This is something Vatican II distinctly emphasized. As a coworker with his bishop, the priest shares in the mission that Christ entrusted to his apostles — the mission to preach salvation to the ends of the earth.[57] "All priests must have the mind and the heart of missionaries — open to the needs of the Church and the world," John Paul taught. "They should have at heart, in their prayers and particularly at the Eucharistic Sacrifice, the concern of the Church for all of humanity."[58]

In many ways, priests today face a situation no different than that faced by the missionaries of America's first evangelization. As those first missionaries were, the priest today is a man of uncommon generosity. In his priestly vocation he has set out on a life's journey in response to the call of our Lord, with courage and holy daring following in Christ's footsteps to be a shepherd to his people. Entrusting himself to Christ in faith and hope, he has left everything behind — family and security — to love God and to serve him.

Priests spend themselves daily in love to bring men and women into Christ's saving truth and presence. And in this they open their hearts to their brothers and sisters in all their joys and anguish, sharing in every aspect of their people's lives — baptizing and marrying; anointing and burying; comforting and teaching; defending their dignity and praying for their sanctity. In all things, the priest stands *in persona Christi*, lending his voice and hands to Christ as he continues to speak, heal, and give himself to his people through the ministry of his priests.

And we share with our priestly forebears many common trials, burdens, and anxieties. Here in North America in the early years of the twenty-first century we do not face the diabolical anti-clericalism experienced by St. Roque González in sixteenth-century Paraguay or by the Mexican clergy during the *Cristero* rebellion of the early twentieth century. But the priest today ministers in a dominant culture that is sometimes hostile and sometimes callously indifferent to the truths and values of the Gospel.

In this culture, the priest often faces suspicion, ridicule, and incomprehension. In the wake of the scandal involving the sexual abuse of minors, even the vast majority of priests who did no wrong experience shame at the crimes of their brothers and labor under the resulting loss of trust and esteem for the priesthood, even within the Church.

The priest today also ministers under the heavy burdens imposed by the shortage of priestly coworkers. This means he often suffers the very human emotions of overwork, fatigue, loneliness, and that sense that his work is not fully understood or appreciated. He experiences, too, temptations peculiar to American culture, especially the temptation to an excessive activism. These temptations grow in part out of the culture of work in America, which tends towards a frenetic workaholism, and defines "success" in terms of programs and material results.

The concerns expressed in *Presbyterorum Ordinis* remain valid. Especially in the American context, priests face "considerable danger of dissipating their energy," and must struggle to "coordinate and balance their interior life with feverish outward activity."[59] Again, this situation is not new. Many priests today, not to mention many bishops, would recognize Bishop Joseph P. Machebeuf's description of his ministry in 1876:

> On Saturday and Sunday, I am a priest and bishop to confess, preach, and officiate, etc. On Monday and the rest of the week I am a banker, contractor, architect, mason, collector — in a word, a little of everything.... [This] exactly describes my position in Colorado, where

everything must be built up from the bottom. I wonder I am not sick, but I have not the time. A real American has no time to be sick. No time to eat or sleep. No time for anything except the "go ahead."[60]

Bishop Machebeuf, the first bishop of Denver, is another hero of America's first evangelization. Along with his fellow French priest, Jean Baptiste Lamy (later the first Archbishop of Santa Fe), he sailed from his homeland to bring the Gospel to the New World. They preached and celebrated the sacraments throughout North America, traveling by horseback and wagon from Ohio to Santa Fe to Denver, and many points in between. They faced shipwreck, diseases, hostilities, and hardship. They experienced menacing run-ins with the Apache Indians and others opposed to the values of the Gospel — gunfighters, gamblers, rustlers, claim-jumpers.

Yet in the stories of their lives, and in their sermons and writings, we see evidence of a keen apostolic fervor and idealism. We see their delight in having been found worthy to be called to sacrificial service of Christ and the Church. In one three-month period, then-Father Machebeuf traveled more than 1,500 miles over mountains, valleys, and plains — celebrating Mass everywhere he went on a little altar on the back of his horse-drawn buggy. During that trip he braved an outbreak of smallpox that was ravaging many of the small communities he visited and, at one point, his buggy was driven off the road and over a cliff. Describing the events in a letter to his sister, he wrote: "Thus you see the life of a missionary, and how Providence protects him in all sorts of dangers. Why should we fear sickness and death?"[61]

Archbishop Lamy likewise had a lively faith in Providence, and he preached often of holiness and the virtues. "The saints' example ought to animate us," he said in a sermon he preached in Spanish in Santa Fe in 1876. "For we also are called to be saints — and not only *can* we, but we *ought* to; for it is our duty, our obligation. The God we serve is holy, and he wishes to be served by holy persons. So we have a duty to make every effort to imitate the saints and to make ourselves holy as they did."[62]

In a sermon delivered in 1875, Archbishop Lamy spoke of perseverance.

> To reconcile ourselves with God and resolve to lead a virtuous life is good. But it is not all. We must besides persevere in our fidelity to God, for our divine Savior has said, "He who shall persevere to the end shall be saved."... Without perseverance we cannot succeed even in worldly affairs. Much less can we expect to succeed in the most important affair of our salvation. Without energy, constancy, perseverance, we cannot expect to save our souls and to secure the greatest of all rewards, the glory of heaven.[63]

The Courage and the Truth of the Priesthood

In moral theology, perseverance has traditionally been treated as a part of the virtue of fortitude.[64] And in the lives of Lamy, Machebeuf, Margil, along with the other great missionary saints and martyrs, fortitude or courage is the virtue most vital to their spirituality and identity.

And I do not hesitate to say that we must cultivate this virtue first and above all others in the lives of priests and seminarians today. Fortitude is the virtue that makes the cultivation of all the other virtues possible. It is the virtue of Christian self-possession. Fortitude is the virtue that fights off fear and enables a man to know who he is and who God has called him to be. By fortitude we have the courage of self-examination and the power to master our passions and appetites and to withstand temptations, enticements, and fears. Only by the virtue of fortitude will the priest be able to maintain the unity of life that is so fragile in this era when the number of priests is declining and the demands on his ministry seem unending.

It is true that in classical presentations of the virtues, pre-eminence is usually given to the virtue of prudence. Following Aquinas, Pieper argues that prudence is "the mold and 'mother' of all the other cardinal virtues.... In other words, none but the prudent man can be just, brave, and temperate, and the good man is good in so far as he is prudent."[65] I certainly would not dispute this from the standpoint of either moral theology or spiritual direction. Nonetheless, I am convinced that in the circumstances of the present day it is not out of order to say that we need to cultivate fortitude as the foundation of a heroic and missionary priestly identity and spirituality.

I find myself in agreement with Ambrose, the first great Christian philosopher of the virtues. Writing in the fourth century, the bishop of Milan said that fortitude is "a loftier virtue than the rest but it is also one that never stands alone":

> Fortitude ... wages war in conjunction with the virtues, and alone defends the beauty of all the virtues, and guards their powers of discernment. It wages relentless war against all the vices. It is unbowed by toil, brave to endure dangers, stern against pleasures, hardened against allurements, to which it knows not how to lend an ear.... It cares not for money and flies from avarice as from a plague that destroys all virtue.[66]

Fortitude fights fear, and we in the clergy have much to fear. I have already alluded to some of the challenges facing priests today. We live in a culture that, while it does not persecute believers, sharply restricts expressions of the Christian faith and pressures believers to abandon core principles of their faith in order to "get along." In addition, priests today face the daily temptations of a culture that promotes material comfort, morals and ethics without responsibility, and which questions eternal values and lifelong commitments.

To proclaim the Gospel in this climate, we need all the virtues, but especially the virtue of fortitude. In one of his early addresses to priests, John Paul II said:

> With all the power of persuasion at my command, I say to each one: Priest, be what you are, without restrictions, without illusions, without compromise in the face of God and your conscience.... Have always the courage of the truth of your priesthood.[67]

The courage of the truth of your priesthood! This is what priests, and those training for the priesthood, need today. Yet as with the other virtues, fortitude is no longer well understood or even discussed. As I mentioned, our moral teaching has tended to emphasize Church laws and precepts and the obligations of believers and confessors. While such teaching is certainly essential, we can question whether these areas have been stressed to the detriment or exclusion of other key dimensions of moral character development.

Indeed, I believe we now recognize that the Church's moral laws and commandments can be fully appreciated only in light of a discipleship centered on the imitation of Christ and the love of the Creator who has first loved us.[68] The goal of priestly renewal must be the ideal proposed by New Testament spirituality — namely, the formation of what St. Paul called "the mind of Christ," through the love of God and imitation of the virtues of Christ.[69]

In his important work, which aims at returning Christian morality to the virtue-centered approach of St. Thomas, Dominican Father Servais Pinckaers has observed:

> We will look in vain for a simple allusion, still less for a full treatment of the virtue of courage in many of the manuals [of moral theology]. Courage is not a matter of obligation. Yet it is numbered among the four cardinal

virtues. St. Thomas associated it with the ideal of martyrdom, the inspiration of the early centuries of Christianity. *Everyone knows from experience how great is the need for courage throughout our moral life.*[70]

I underline this last point. Courage or fortitude is essential for the moral growth and development of the Christian — and especially for the priest. We need to recover this idea of fortitude as the virtue that makes possible the practice of all the others. We need to see fortitude as the defender of the beauty and the glory of the life of virtue. And we need to see the inseparable relationship of fortitude with the central mystery of our faith, the cross and resurrection of Jesus Christ. Father Romanus Cessario, another Dominican who in recent years has helped us to appreciate the virtues as the centerpiece of Christian living, has written:

> The mystery of the cross gives a central place in Christian virtue to martyrdom and the patient endurance of suffering for the sake of Christ, that is, to fortitude and with it to nonviolence rather than the aggressiveness which predominated in the Greek notion of virtue.[71]

The Lord's Cross and the Beginning of Courage

In the pages that follow, I want to begin a retrieval of Christian fortitude as the centerpiece of a priestly spirituality centered on the mystery of the cross. To understand and cultivate fortitude in the priestly life, we must first understand how Christian fortitude is radically different from the ideal of the virtue found in the Hellenistic world. Incidentally, the associated Hellenistic notions of courage, strength, and manhood are those found in the secular world today. So we need to discuss the differences there, too, especially as they pertain to our priestly identity.

To understand the radical newness of Christian fortitude, we need to return to the source, to the roots of Christian fortitude in the Gospel. But we also need to see how those roots were prepared in the Old Testament. This means reading the Old Testament in the light of Christ, as the author of the letter to the Hebrews did, seeing how "faith conquered kingdoms [and] won strength out of weakness."[72] Only then can we understand Gospel fortitude, which is a sharing in the power of the cross of Christ, who overcame the world.[73]

Finally we need to see how St. Thomas Aquinas synthesized the classical and evangelical ideals of fortitude in his Christian philosophy of the nature and destiny of man. As Father Cessario rightly observes, "More than any other classical Christian author, Aquinas develops a profoundly systematic reflection on the virtue of fortitude."[74] Thomas's systematic reflection, I believe, holds great potential for priests today, especially when read in light of the sources of Christian fortitude in sacred Scripture and in light of the "science of the saints," who embody the virtue in heroic ways.

This is the course I will travel in the chapters that follow. But we must keep in mind that our aim is not a detached academic study of the virtue. We need to better understand fortitude in order to better live it in the service of the Kingdom of God. Through our reflection on the witness of Scripture and the tradition we want to enter more deeply into the mystery of Christ, the mystery of the cross.

Our priestly vocation unfolds under the sign of this mystery, the sign of Christ's redemptive sacrifice which we renew each day in the sacrifice of the Eucharist. If the mystery of the cross gives a central place to the virtue of fortitude, the prayerful cultivation of this virtue promises to lead the priest deeper into the heart of his vocation, which is nothing other than the taking up of his cross in imitation of Christ. Again, we can see this clearly in the lives of the saints. As Ambrose said:

> For this cause, then, that we might learn these diverse virtues, "a Son was given us, whose beginning was upon his shoulder" (Isa. 9:6). That "beginning" is *the Lord's cross — the beginning of strong courage.* By this beginning, a way has been opened for the holy martyrs to enter the sufferings of the holy war.[75]

Contemplation of the mystery of the cross is the beginning of strong courage for the priest. In fact, growth in the virtue of fortitude means cultivating the spirit of the cross in the life of the priest. And as the saints all knew, fortitude is essential for the ascetical struggle, the holy warfare of the soul that we are called to.

Venerable Father Antonio Margil used to sign all of his letters, *La misma nada,* "Nothingness itself." Developing this humility, this consciousness of our dependence upon Christ — that without him we can do nothing, that in our lives and ministries we must decrease as he must increase — must be a high priority in our spiritual formation of priests. This consciousness grows from the strong courage of one who has reflected deeply on the meaning of the cross.

And in his famous "Abalado," a song of praise he composed to catechize the native peoples of the Americas, Father Antonio taught them to pray these words, which should become the daily prayer of the priest who would cultivate the spiritual gift and virtue of fortitude:

> O dearest Jesus,
> To you I give my heart,
> Imprint on it, dear Lord,
> Your most holy Passion.[76]

CHAPTER 2

All Things in Him Who Strengthens Me

Power, Manhood, and the Priesthood

FATHER WALTER J. CISZEK, S.J., was a tough kid. In fact, that is what they called him in Shenandoah, Pennsylvania, when he was growing up in the early 1910s — "a tough." It was not a compliment. The young Walter was a bully, a gang leader, and a street fighter. He had no interest in school and many days could not be bothered to attend. He played hooky so much that, while he was still in his parish grammar school, his frustrated father marched him down to the police station and urged them, without success, to ship his son off to reform school.

One day his father gave him some money to take the train to Boy Scout camp. Walter took the money and went off to an amusement park instead. He spent all his money there and did not have any left to pay the fare to get home. So he decided to hitch a ride by hanging onto the outside of one of the train cars. It seemed like a good idea until the train passed through a tunnel. Walter was nearly crushed against one of the tunnel walls.

Walter was "an unlikely priest," as he titled the first chapter of his memoir. Yet following his eighth-grade year, to everyone's surprise, he announced his intention to join the seminary. Even in seminary, while his devotion to the faith was unquestioned, he was branded as tough, stubborn, and fiercely self-reliant.

He made a point of getting up every day before everyone else, at 4:30 a.m., and running five miles around the lake on the seminary grounds, regardless of the weather. Always striving to be "stronger" and "better" than his classmates, he made sure he performed the most difficult penances and ascetic disciplines. One Lent he ate only bread and water for the entire forty days. Another time he gave up meat for the whole year.

Then one day without warning, three years before he was to be ordained, he quit the diocesan seminary to join the Jesuits — even though it would mean seven more years of training and formation. "I asked no one's advice," Walter recalled. "I just prayed and fought with myself — and finally decided, since it was so hard, I would do it." His proud, hardheaded style almost got him kicked out of the Jesuit novitiate. But he continued with his practice of "going without certain things and of undertaking annoying jobs, just to condition myself to do the harder thing and to strengthen my will." To earn his philosophy degree, he wrote his thesis on a subject he seemed to have spent his lifetime studying — "On the Training of the Will."

Walter was ordained as a Jesuit and then, in response to an urgent appeal from Pope Pius XII to the Jesuits, he volunteered for service in communist Russia as a secret missionary. This required four more years of arduous training in Russian language, history, and liturgy. And the assignment he took was dangerous. He was to be "an underground" priest.

The Catholic faith had been outlawed violently in Soviet Russia — churches had been destroyed, seminaries closed, the faithful scattered, and bishops and priests tortured and locked up in concentration camps. Living under an assumed name in a logging town in the Ural Mountains, for a year Father Ciszek worked as a logger while secretly celebrating Mass, hearing confessions, and performing the other spiritual and pastoral works of a priest.

But in 1941 he was caught and charged with being a "Vatican spy." Held in Moscow's infamous Lubianka prison, he was brutally interrogated by his captors for more than a year, until finally he broke down and signed a false confession. He was sentenced to fifteen years hard labor in one of the Soviet Union's most notorious *gulags*. He would spend nearly two dozen years in isolation and suffering in Soviet prisons, including five years in Siberia, not far from the Arctic Circle. His family gave him up for dead. The Jesuits even celebrated a Mass for the repose of his soul.

When he was finally released in 1963, he remembered, not the sufferings he had endured at the hands of his persecutors, but the shame and weakness he had felt in signing that false confession. At first, he said, he had been ashamed at his weakness. He blamed himself for not having been strong enough to withstand the tortures. He blamed God for abandoning him:

> My will had failed; I had proved to be nowhere near the man I thought I was. I had yielded ... to fear, to threats, to the thought of death.... I did not spare God from [my] reproaches. Why had he failed me at the critical juncture? Why had he not sustained my strength and my nerve? Why had he not inspired me to speak out boldly? Why had he not shielded me by his grace from the fear of death?

But in the dark days that followed his signing of that false confession, Father Ciszek prayed hard and made an intense examination of conscience. With the help of God's grace, he came to some life-changing understandings about himself. He came to see that he had approached his arrest and interrogation as he had everything else in his life — as a contest of wills and a test of his own powers and strength.

What he came to realize was that it was not the Soviets who were contesting with him, it was God. And it was not his physical strength and will-power that were being tested. It was his confidence in God that had been put on trial — and been found wanting. Father Ciszek had put too much stock in his own powers, trusted too much in his own abilities. Although he prayed often, he realized that he had never really prayed out of any sense of true thanksgiving, out of any sense of his "need" for God. He compared himself to the Pharisee in Jesus' parable, who came to the Temple to thank God that he was "not like other men — extortioners, unjust, adulterers."

> The answer was a single word: *I*. I was ashamed because I knew in my heart that I had tried to do too much on my own, and I had asked for God's help but had really believed in my own ability to avoid evil and to meet every challenge. I had spent much time in prayer over the years, I had come to appreciate and thank God for his providence and care of men and of all men, but I had never really abandoned myself to it. In a way, I had been thanking God all the while that I was not like the rest of men, that he had given me a good physique, steady nerves, and a strong will, and that with these physical graces given by God I would continue to do his will at all times and to the best of *my* ability.... The sense of guilt and shame I felt was rooted in my failure to put grace ahead of nature, my failure to trust primarily in God rather than in my own powers.[1]

The lesson that Father Ciszek learned under such harrowing circumstances is a lesson that must be learned on some level by every Christian — and in a special way by every man who desires to be a priest. It is a lesson in humility and trust in the Gospel, a lesson in self-abandonment to the Word of God.

Ultimately, what we all must learn is that no matter what our gifts, abilities, and training, no matter how hard we work, and no matter what we are able to achieve, everything is a gift from God in Christ Jesus, and God alone is the true source of our strength and power in this life. Learning this lesson is the beginning of growing in Christian character. And, as we explore in this chapter, for this growth in character, we need the virtue of courage or fortitude.

Apart from Me You Can Do Nothing

I said this lesson in the true source of our strength is especially important for priests to learn. Why? Because the priest is not ordained for himself. In the image of Christ, he is the man for others, set apart for this service in a personal way *by* Jesus and *for* Jesus. The priest has no agenda of his own and no mission of his own. Everything he does is to fulfill the mission that God gave to Jesus, a mission that Jesus in turn handed on to the apostles of his Church after his resurrection, and they in turned handed on to bishops and their priest coworkers for every succeeding generation: "As the Father has sent me, even so I send you" (John 20:21).[2]

Pope John Paul II once wrote: "This priesthood is destined to last in endless succession throughout history."[3] Until Christ returns, the priest is to continue his mission, bringing to this fallen world the good news of salvation — of the forgiveness of sins, of our adoption as children of God, and of the promise of the resurrection and eternal life. The powers and authority to undertake that mission, given first to the apostles, are now given to every priest at his ordination through the laying on of the bishop's hands:

He who hears you, hears me. (Luke 10:16; Matt. 10:40)

Make disciples of all nations, baptizing them... [and] teaching them to observe all that I have commanded you. (Matt. 28:19–20)

This is my body.... Do this in remembrance of me. (Luke 22:20)

If you forgive the sins of any, they are forgiven; if you retain the sins of any, they are retained. (John 20:23)

Whatever you bind on earth shall be bound in heaven, and whatever you loose on earth shall be loosed in heaven. (Matt. 18:18)

These are truly amazing powers — to preach and teach in Jesus' name; to forgive sins in his name and to make binding decisions regarding the government of his Church on earth; to make men and women children of God in baptism; and finally, to bring them into communion with the risen Body and Blood of Jesus Christ himself.

These extraordinary powers are given to no one else on earth but to Christ's bishops and priests. In the beautiful words of the fourth-century doctor of the Church, St. John Chrysostom, we see the high place the priestly vocation holds in God's plan for the Church and the world:

What great honor the grace of the Spirit has granted to priests! They who make their abode on earth are entrusted with the administration of the things that are in heaven. They have received an authority that God has not given to angels or archangels.... For indeed, what is it but all manner of heavenly authority which he has given to them... [powers] without which it is not possible to obtain either our own salvation, or the good things which have been promised to us.

For if no one can enter into the Kingdom of Heaven unless he is regenerated through water and the Spirit (John 3:5), and if he who does not eat the flesh of the Lord and drink his blood is excluded from eternal life

(John 6:53–54), and if all these things are accomplished only by means of these holy hands — I mean the hands of the priest — then how will anyone, without these, be able to escape the fires of hell or to win those crowns which are reserved for the victorious?[4]

We do not tend to speak this way about priests anymore. We are much more sensitive to the human character of the priesthood — that the priest, though "chosen from among men," nonetheless struggles against the same weaknesses and sinful tendencies as those whom he serves before God.[5]

This accent today is correct. The priest, before anything else, is a man. The basis of all priestly formation — spiritual, intellectual, pastoral — must be the formation of priests and seminarians in the human virtues, especially in such qualities as "goodness of heart, sincerity, strength and constancy of mind, zealous pursuit of justice, affability, and others."[6]

As I said in the first chapter and continue to emphasize throughout this book: God does not call only "perfect" men to the priesthood. Such men do not exist except in heaven. But the man who would be a priest must be committed to being a hearer and a keeper of the Word that he himself would proclaim: "Repent, and believe in the Gospel."[7] He must be committed to ongoing, lifelong conversion and transformation in Christ. In this, he is like every other Christian.

At the same time, what Chrysostom said also remains true: In the divine economy, in God's plan of salvation, the priest plays a role that no one else can play. And for that role the priest is given powers that no one else — in the Church or anywhere else on earth — can possess. This dimension of the priesthood is not in tension with the human dimension. Indeed, the priest's human personality should serve as a "bridge" for the encounter with Jesus Christ that the priest brings through his ministry.[8]

We do not want to put priests on a pedestal for veneration. The roots of clerical mind-sets and habits in the Church lie in this kind of exaggerated regard for priestly power and authority. Yet I would agree with those who say that in recent years we have tilted too far in the other direction, emphasizing "the priesthood of all believers" while forgetting the special calling of the ordained priesthood and its place in God's economy of salvation.[9]

In training seminarians and in the ongoing formation of priests, we need a balanced understanding of the human and divine aspects of the ordained state. For that, we need a proper understanding of the nature and source of the priest's powers and authority. This is why I said that growth in priestly character must begin in learning the lesson that Father Ciszek learned in Lubianka — that his strength was not his own.

The Power and Infirmity of Apostolic Ministry

This lesson is also key to understanding and acquiring the virtue of fortitude. We look at that more closely in the chapters that follow. Here we want to focus on the unique source of priestly power and strength in Christ Jesus. The priest needs the humility to remember that he is nothing without the grace he has been given. He "called us with a holy calling, not in virtue of our works, but in virtue of his own purpose and the grace which he gave us."[10]

The first lesson of fortitude for the priest is what Christ told the apostles: "Apart from me you can do nothing."[11] This is not to reduce the priest to being a passive vessel or conduit for the work of Christ. Far from it. The priest is called to use and cultivate his natural gifts, to develop his strengths, to work to overcome his weaknesses, and to master his passions.

The human effort of the priest is critical. Certainly no one would say that Jesus in his earthly ministry was anything less than bold, resourceful, and strong. Yet Jesus said of himself the same thing that he told the apostles: "The Son can do nothing of his own accord.... I seek not my own will but the will of him who sent me."[12]

The priest's identity with Christ must mirror the identity of Christ with his Father. These words of Pope Benedict XVI show us the depths of that identity and the meaning of the priestly vocation:

> This "nothing" that the disciples share with Jesus (see John 5:19) expresses at one and the same time both *the power and the infirmity of the apostolic ministry.* By themselves, of their own strength, they can do none of those things that apostles must do. How could they of their own accord say, "I forgive you your sins"? How could they say, "This is my body"? How could they perform the imposition of the hands and say, "Receive the Holy Spirit"?
>
> None of these things that constitute apostolic activity are done by one's own authority. But this expropriation of their very powers constitutes a mode of communion with Jesus, who is wholly from the Father, with him all things and nothing without him. Their own "*nihil posse,*" their own inability to do anything, draws them into a community of mission with Jesus. Such a ministry, in which a man does and gives through a divine communication what he could never do and give on his own, is called by the tradition of the Church a sacrament.
>
> If Church usage calls ordination to the ministry of priesthood a sacrament, the following is meant: this man is in no way performing functions for which he is highly qualified by his own natural ability, nor is he doing the things that please him most and that are most profitable. On the contrary: the one who receives the sacrament is sent to give what he cannot give of his own strength; he is

sent to act in the person of another, to be his living instrument.... the voice and the hands of Christ in the world.

This gift of himself, this renunciation and forgetfulness of self, does not, however, destroy the man; rather it leads to true human maturity because it assimilates him to the trinitarian mystery and it brings to life the image according to which we were created. Since we were created in the image of the Trinity, he who loses himself will find himself.[13]

In this passage we find the essence of the theology and spirituality of the priesthood. We will return to these ideas throughout this book. First, the Pope reminds us that the priesthood is an *apostolic ministry* — that is, the priest shares in the responsibilities and mission that Jesus gave to the apostles. The powers the priest is given are the same as those given to the apostles. These powers are not given for their own sake, but for the sake of Christ's mission, for the sake of what he was *sent* into the world to do. To say that the priesthood is an apostolic ministry is to remind ourselves that the priest is always one who is *sent* (which, as we know, is the meaning of the word "apostle").

By its very nature the priestly vocation is *missionary*. The priest is the man who is sent on a mission from God. He is an apostle and servant of God as Jesus himself was an "apostle" and servant of the Father.[14] Sharing in this apostolic ministry, the priest shares in the apostles' special friendship with Jesus Christ. "No longer do I call you servants, for the servant does not know what his Master is doing; but I have called you friends, for all that I have heard from my Father I have made known to you."[15] The priest is a friend of Jesus Christ. That means he knows and shares in the mission that the Father sent Christ to do.[16]

This is what Benedict means by "*the power and infirmity* of the apostolic ministry." This concept is essential for grasping the meaning of Holy Orders as a sacrament and for under-standing the true nature of the priest's powers and authority. As Benedict indicates, everything the priest *is* and everything the priest *is able to do* comes from his communion with Jesus Christ. His identity and power come to him in the sacrament. In the essence of his priestly nature he is the "living instrument ... the voice and the hands of Christ in the world," as Benedict says so beautifully.

Weakness and the Essence of True "Manhood"

The priest finds the meaning of his apostolic ministry — and the power of his ministry — in his *infirmity*, in his weak-ness. This was the experience of the first apostolic ministers. "I will not boast, except of my weakness," St. Paul said. "For when I am weak, then I am strong."[17] Paul experienced Christ giving him strength in his weakness through the power of the Holy Spirit.[18] He understood this "power in infirmity" as rooted in the cross of Christ — the cross being the sign of weakness and humiliation by which God showed his power over the ultimate enemy, death.

Yet, as Paul realized, the Christian belief in strength through weakness was seen as "foolishness" by many in the sur-rounding culture. In the Roman world, the idea of "manliness" (*virtus* in Latin) was closely associated with notions of rugged personal independence and aggressive physical strength.[19] The measure of a "man" was his capacity to do for himself without needing the help of others. A true man was able especially to hold his own against others in physical combat.

In that cultural context, for Christians like Paul to suggest that one could be strong in infirmity or weakness sounded crazy and ridiculous. From the beginning, Christians were often ridi-culed as weaklings and fools who were indifferent to the concerns of this world and who would rather be dead than alive. Writing in the early third century, Tertullian reported that Christians were dismissed as "exiles from life" and "useless persons."[20]

This critique has been carried forward into our own day by way of the scorn of Friedrich Nietzsche, who argued that Christianity made men weak, and Karl Marx, who called the faith an "opiate" that numbed believers to the world's injustices. The classic expression of this criticism came from Niccolò Machiavelli, who said our religion prepared men "for suffering rather than vigorous action."[21]

"The unbeliever has always reproached Christianity for making men unmanly," concludes Father A. Gauthier, the Dominican moral theologian.[22] We should note that while this reproach is made against Christianity in general, it has long been used to slander priests in particular. The priest, by foreswearing sexual relations in the service of the Kingdom of God, is wrongly imagined to be a softer, weaker kind of man. This is still a kind of undercurrent in polemics against priestly celibacy — again, the implication being that voluntary celibacy somehow renders the priest less of a "man." Such criticisms are based on profoundly mistaken notions — not only about the gift of self in priestly celibacy, but about the true nature of strength, power, and manhood.

There has not been enough study or writing on the nature of authentic masculinity or manhood as it is understood in the Christian tradition. For many reasons, few today would even dare attempt "a rough sketch of man as differentiated from woman," as Jesuit Father Karl Rahner tried to do in the 1960s.[23] This is unfortunate because the Church's magisterial teaching presumes a commonsense perspective that recognizes distinctions between men and women and between masculinity and femininity. This perspective was expressed well by the German lay theologian, Ida Friederike Görres:

Prudence, justice, fortitude, and temperance express themselves differently in men and women and are evoked in different situations. The priest must personify their male aspect, for instance in his role of father.[24]

Our formation efforts today should reflect this common-sense perspective. Specifically, we need to pay attention to how priests are meant to live and personify the cardinal virtues *as men*. As Pope Benedict has said: "Christ needs priests who are mature, virile, capable of cultivating an authentic spiritual paternity."[25]

This focus on an authentic manhood and masculinity is important for priestly spirituality. It is related intrinsically to Christ's reservation of the priestly vocation to men. We have been talking about the apostolic calling as the salvation-historical basis of the priesthood. Following the example of Jesus, who chose twelve men to be his apostles, the Church from New Testament times has understood this apostolic calling to be expressly reserved to "men" (*andres* in Greek; *vir* in Latin).[26] The Church's magisterial documents presume that there is a profound sacramental symbolism at work in "the economy of revelation."

> That is why we can never ignore the fact that Christ is a man (*Christum virum esse* in Latin)... and therefore... in actions which demand the character of ordination and in which Christ himself, the author of the covenant, the bridegroom and head of the Church, is represented exercising his ministry of salvation ... his role ... must be taken by a man.[27]

Magisterial teaching on the priesthood is based, in part, on "the fact that Christ is a man." This teaching presumes real differences between the sexes, and that these differences of sex have a deep and intimate influence on "man and woman in their profound identity."[28] It follows that a proper and balanced understanding of masculinity and manhood will be vital in the formation of true priestly identity and character in "the spirit and style of Jesus the Good Shepherd."[29]

Society today, much like the Roman world, provides a powerful "countersign" or "anti-witness" to an authentically Christian masculinity and manhood. By that I mean that the world today still defines "manhood" according to standards not much different than those of the Romans. In many ways, our secular ideals have not changed much since the time of St. Paul. We could say that the "real man," according to the secular world today, is a person quite like the man that Father Ciszek was at first striving to be — proud, with "a good physique and a strong will"; fiercely self-sufficient with no need for others; a fighter, a "tough" guy. This type was already described well in Plutarch's *Life of Coriolanus*, written about A.D. 75:

> [I]n those days Rome held in highest honor that phase of virtue which concerns itself with warlike and military achievements, and evidence of this may be found in the only Latin word for *virtue*, which signifies really *manly valor*; they made valor, a specific form of virtue, stand for virtue in general.[30]

Cicero, too, testifies to this Roman ideal. In fact, he points to courage, or fortitude as the central meaning of *virtus*, or "manliness." As he points out: "Although all the right affections of the soul are classed under the name of virtue, the truth is that this is not properly the name of them all, but rather they all have their name from that leading virtue which is superior to all the rest; for the name 'virtue' comes from *vir*, a man, and the peculiar distinction of a man is courage."[31]

What Plutarch and Cicero observed about Rome we could observe about American society today. "Manliness" is still largely equated with a brute strength, a rugged independence from others, and an aggressive sexuality. Even a simple look at popular culture, advertising, sports, and entertainment could serve to prove this. If we were to look at the tragic crisis of fatherhood and commitment in our society, we would see even more deeply how flawed our models of manhood have become.

I cannot make such an analysis here. My point is that we must be attentive to these cultural realities. Seminarians are products of this environment, and priests are forced to reckon with its implications daily. In our formation efforts, we must stress the development of an authentic priestly virility and spiritual paternity.

This dimension of priestly identity is expressed most distinctly in the discipline of celibacy. The apostolic roots of the discipline are clear,[32] as is its symbolism of the mystical marriage of Christ and the Church. The meaning of celibacy as a complete gift of self, a total consecration of the priest to Christ and the service of his kingdom is also well known. Celibacy is a core aspect of the missionary heart of the priesthood.

There are excellent works available on the spiritual and psychological dimensions of celibacy.[33] Here, I would like to concentrate on the issue of celibacy and the "manhood" of the priest. Celibacy is a sign of contradiction in our overly sexualized society. But the priest does not become less of a "man" by giving up the possibilities of marriage and fatherhood. In his relationships, the priest is always a man — a brother, a son, and a friend — even as he assumes the responsibilities of spiritual fatherhood in the Church.

And by his faithful and joyful embrace of celibacy, he points the way to an authentic understanding of manhood — one that transcends the merely physical attractions and desires of our bodily nature and looks to the establishment of intimate emotional and spiritual bonds. The gift of celibacy cannot be lived apart from a plan of priestly life that is aimed at growth in the virtues. As the priest perseveres in that plan of life, he will find that he is strengthened in his struggles against sin and that he experiences a growing freedom and simplicity in his relationships with women.[34]

The priest in most cases has grown up with sisters and is likely to have a particularly strong bond to his mother. In the family of the Church, the priest recognizes all men and women as brothers and sisters in Christ. This familial unity created by baptism should shape the priest's affective friendships with both men and women. In the case of women, he should follow the advice that St. Paul gave to Timothy: "Treat... older women like mothers, younger women like sisters, in all purity."[35]

In order to begin this process of spiritual growth, the priest must first learn the lessons of Father Ciszek. Through his experience of debasement and torture, Father Ciszek learned what it means to truly be a man. Recall how he expressed his crushing disappointment — he discovered that he was not, "the *man* I thought I was." But in his hour of weakness, he discovered what the Pope has called "the power and infirmity of the apostolic ministry" — the power that comes from abandoning trust in our own abilities, the strength that comes only from the cross, as a divine gift.

He discovered his own authentic manhood in Christ's, not in self-assertion but in self-offering, in laying down his life out of love in imitation of Christ, the "true man." Father Ciszek was able to make a powerful testimony: "Only in God would I put my trust. From then on, I felt stronger and comforted. No matter what the danger I always felt his help and a growing confidence in him."[36]

To repeat and conclude: This attitude is the beginning of the new and intimate relationship with Jesus Christ that characterizes priestly ministry. As Jesus did not seek his own will but only the will of the One who sent him,[37] so too, the priest seeks only to be a faithful "servant of God" and an "ambassador for Christ."[38] In this, the priest will know the promise of Christ, who told St. Paul: "My grace is sufficient for you, for my power is made perfect in weakness."[39] He will feel the confidence that Father Ciszek came to feel, the confidence that St. Paul felt in his priestly ministry: "I can do all things in him who strengthens me."[40]

Father Ciszek had one insight that I wished he had developed further. He said that in the face of his interrogator's threats, "In that moment, I had not seen death as God sees it or as I professed to believe it."[41] This is very wise. I believe that on some level the fear of death is ultimately what keeps us from bearing witness to our Lord, from living his Gospel.

This is why fortitude is central to growth in Christian character — and specifically priestly character. As we explore in the chapters that follow, fortitude is the gift of fearlessness in the face of death. And, as we will see, Christian fortitude, as an essential component of authentic Christian manhood, is something radically new, something radically different than the conceptions of fortitude found in the ancient world or in our world today.

CHAPTER 3

Contempt of Death and the Crown of Life

The Radical Newness of Christian Fortitude

In the first generation of the Church, even their opponents and persecutors could not help noticing that there was something distinctive, even something they had to admire about Christians. They remarked on it frequently in the records that survive. The Christians, they said, were generous, lived disciplined lives, and were courageous, even when being tortured in the most cruel ways.

In those days it did seem like the Roman rulers were in some sick competition to find ever more hideous ways to make Christians suffer. "New tortures were continually invented, as if they were endeavoring by surpassing one another to gain prizes in a contest," according to Eusebius, the fourth-century bishop and historian.[1]

Often bishops and priests were seized first by authorities because they were the leaders of the community. And there are many stories of bravery among the first Christian clergy. Vocations were forged in the crucible of suffering.

I am moved by the story of the young African, Celerinus. In the winter of 249, during the persecution of the Emperor Decius, Celerinus was jailed in Rome, sharing a dank cell with a number of priests. Though only twenty at the time, he already knew the high cost of Christian discipleship. He came from a family of martyrs, with his grandmother and two uncles having been killed for the faith.

Celerinus was brought before Decius. And when he refused to offer sacrifices to the Roman gods, he was placed in leg irons. His punishment meant being forced to lie on the ground on his back, his legs chained so that they were stretched as far apart as possible. He was held in this position, unable to move, for nineteen days. After he was finally released, he was never again able to walk straight or without pain. He presented himself to St. Cyprian, the bishop of Carthage, and some time later was ordained.

"Illustrious for his acts of bravery and for his virtues, he has been joined to our clergy, not by the election of man, but by the favor of God," Cyprian said in a letter to the priests of Carthage. Of Celerinus's captivity, Cyprian said: "Though his body was in bondage, his spirit remained unfettered and free. His flesh grew emaciated by prolonged hunger and thirst, but his soul, living by faith and courage, God nourished with spiritual sustenance. He lay in the midst of sufferings, stronger than those sufferings.... He was in bonds, mightier than those who bound him."[2]

Another inspiring story from these early days is that of St. Ignatius, the bishop of Antioch. Not much is known about Ignatius. He was arrested during the persecution of the Emperor Trajan, sometime between the years 98 and 117. He wrote seven letters to various churches while he was being carted in a small cage to Rome for trial and execution. These letters are among the treasures of Christian literature. In one, he described his feelings about the prospect of being fed to wild beasts before a jeering crowd in Rome.

All the way from Syria to Rome I am fighting wild beasts, on land and sea, by day and night, chained as I am to ten leopards, that is, a detachment of soldiers who prove themselves the more malevolent for kindness shown them. Yet in the school of this abuse I am more and more *trained in discipleship....* Fire, cross, struggles with wild beasts, wrenching of bones, mangling of limbs, crunching the whole body, cruel tortures inflicted by the devil — let them come upon me, provided only I make my way to Jesus Christ…. *Him I seek who died for us…. Once arrived there, I shall be a man. Permit me to be an imitator of my suffering God.*[3]

In reading their own writings and contemporary writings about them, we are struck by the martyrs' confident sense that to imitate Jesus was to be truly human, to really be a man. We are struck by their calm and self-composure. Cyprian and other early writers attributed this quality of the martyrs to *fortitude,* the virtue of courage.

When the Roman soldiers wanted to nail the saintly bishop Polycarp to the stake so that he would not resist being burned alive, the 90-year-old bishop assured them that this was not necessary — that God would give him the strength he needed: "Leave aside these nails," Polycarp said. "For he who gives me the strength to endure the flames will grant me to stand still without you securing me to the pile."[4]

In his *History of the Church,* Eusebius gives us a beautiful tribute to the faith of countless anonymous Christians:

[N]oble martyrs… strengthened as soldiers of God with patient fortitude, they mocked at death in all its forms; at fire and sword and the torment of crucifixion; at exposure to savage beasts and drowning in the depths of the sea; at the cutting off and searing of limbs, the digging out of eyes, the mutilation of the whole body; lastly, at famine, the labor of the mines, and captivity. All these sufferings they counted better than any earthly good or pleasure, for the love they bore their heavenly King.[5]

Christians did not only go to their death at the hands of their persecutors. Many died nursing and caring for their neighbors in the plagues and epidemics that afflicted the late Empire. The sad fact was that during these outbreaks, many ordinary Romans abandoned their loved ones for dead, fleeing because they were scared they also might be infected with the disease.[6] The Christians stayed. They were not afraid to risk infection and death to comfort and care for their neighbors. "The best of our brothers lost their lives in this manner... priests, deacons, and laymen," Bishop Dionysius of Alexandria wrote in a letter to his people at Easter in A.D. 260, "Death in this form, the result of great piety and strong faith, seems in every way the equal of martyrdom."[7]

Early Church leaders attributed this bravery, too, to the virtue of fortitude. Cyprian, who himself would eventually die a martyr's death, wrote in 251 about the plagues: "We learn not to fear death. These are trainings for us, not deaths; they give to the mind the glory of fortitude; by contempt of death they prepare for the crown."[8]

Stories of the martyrs circulated throughout the early Church and inspired many conversions to the faith. St. Justin was a student of Platonic philosophy in second-century Palestine until he witnessed the faith of the martyrs.

> When I was a disciple of Plato, hearing the accusations brought against the Christians and seeing them so bold when facing death and those things from which men shrink, I said to myself that it was impossible that they could have lived in wickedness and sensuality. For what sensualist or licentious man, whose only thought is to feed his flesh, would welcome death, that he might be deprived of his enjoyments?[9]

Justin became a Christian and one of the first great defenders of the faith and himself eventually wore the martyr's crown. What Justin saw, and what the enemies of the Church saw, was the full flowering of the life of Christian virtue, a life anchored and secured by the virtue of fortitude. Fortitude, we have said, is essentially the courage to face one's own death without fear. As Joseph Pieper wrote: "All fortitude stands in the presence of death. Fortitude is basically readiness to die or, more accurately, readiness to fall, to die, in battle."[10]

That is how the virtue was understood in the ancient world, beginning in the writings of Plato and Aristotle. But from the start there was something radically new about Christian fortitude. The difference was something outside observers could see but never quite make sense of. Writing in A.D. 101, the famous Stoic philosopher, Epictetus, noted that ordinarily only children or mentally disturbed people are able to face death without fear. Christians, by contrast, he said, are fearless *"through habit."* This was an important observation. But Epictetus did not really "get" it. In fact, he thought the Christians' fearlessness in the face of death was just irrational — not guided by "reason" or based on true self-knowledge.[11]

Emperor Marcus Aurelius, another Stoic, and a vicious persecutor of the Christians, had the same basic opinion. In his *Meditations*, he described Christians as irrational and superstitious. Their so-called fearlessness was really nothing of the sort, he argued. It was not an expression of self-discipline or reasoned judgment, but instead was "mere obstinacy" and "tragic show."[12]

It was Marcus's court physician, Galen, who could see that the Christians' approach to death could not be understood except in light of their approach to life.

> Their contempt of death and of its sequel is patent to us every day, and likewise their restraint in cohabitation. For they include not only men but also women who refrain from cohabitating all through their lives; and they also number individuals who, in self-discipline and

self-control in matters of food and drink, and in their keen pursuit of justice, have attained a pitch not inferior to that of genuine philosophers.[13]

Galen here notices a key connection between the ascetical life of Christians — their practice of habits of virtue and self-mastery — and their moral courage in the face of suffering and death. Notice that he identifies, if not by their exact name, the four cardinal virtues — prudence ("self-discipline"), temperance ("self-control"), justice, and fortitude ("contempt of death"). As an aside, it is also interesting that he recognizes celibacy and chastity outside of marriage ("restraint in cohabitation") to be distinguishing marks of these first Christian men and women.

What Galen describes is what Cyprian and Ignatius described — the Christian life as a kind of training that involved physical, mental, and spiritual discipline. Christian discipleship meant leading disciplined lifestyles that rejected the personal immorality widespread in the Empire — the hedonism with regard to food, drink, and entertainment; the licentiousness that tolerated polygamy, incest, various forms of sexual immorality, adultery, contraception, and abortion. These same virtuous habits of life made it possible, when the time came, for Christians to also face their death without anxiety or fear.[14]

Philosophy and Sacred Doctrine

Early Christian thinkers, beginning with St. Paul, appropriated the categories and insights of Greek and Roman philosophy and literature to help teach and explain the new Christian lifestyle.[15] But there was something fundamentally different in their accounts.

We need to keep this in mind as we begin to compare early Christian and classical understandings of fortitude.

There is still much we can learn from studying what classical writers and thinkers had to say. As witnesses to human experience, philosophers and artists can always help us to understand our humanity, what it means to be human in light of the powers of reason that God has given to us. The insights of these witnesses can be powerful and can help us to clarify and better present and defend our understanding of the Christian life.

But we need to be mindful that insights gained from natural philosophy and the humanities are always going to be incomplete. We must test everything against the definitive revelation of Jesus Christ who, in the words of the Second Vatican Council, "fully reveals man to himself and makes his supreme calling clear."[16] In this regard, the viewpoint of Stanley Hauerwaus and Charles Pinches, in their book, *Christians among the Virtues,* is helpful:

> [A]s we believe the great Christian thinkers such as St. Paul and St. Thomas mean to teach us, Greek accounts of the virtues are there to be *used* by Christians, not *built upon.* These name two quite different things. To *use* requires that one apply a thing within a framework significantly other than the one in which it originally appeared, which is precisely what Christianity requires insofar as it refounds human life on the life, death, and resurrection of Jesus Christ, God made flesh.... In the end, then, Christian virtue is not so much initiated action but a response to a love relation with God in Christ. This is why it makes sense for the Christian, Aquinas, to say that true or complete virtue is fundamentally not our own achievement but is rather infused in us by God's grace, which saves us and enables us.[17]

The Christian approach to the classical virtues is transformed by the encounter with Christ. In the beautiful words of St. Thomas Aquinas, "Those who use the works of philosophers in sacred doctrine, by bringing them into the service of faith, do not mix water with wine, but rather change water into wine." Aquinas believed the truths of philosophy, discovered by our natural reason, contained "similitudes" of the higher truths revealed by faith. Genuine insights found in the philosophers can prepare us to understand these higher truths, "just as nature is the preamble to grace."[18] With these more "methodological" questions acknowledged, we can begin to consider the accounts of fortitude found in the ancient philosophers.

Brave Soldiers: Fortitude among the Philosophers

The most systematic and influential account is found in Aristotle's *Nicomachean Ethics*, written 350 years before Christ.[19] After analyzing various types of fear and fearlessness, Aristotle comes to the conclusion that true courage is concerned only with fearlessness in the face of the most fearful things. And the greatest of these most fearful things is death. "Now death is the most fearful of all things," he writes. "For it is the end, and nothing is thought to be any longer either good or bad for the dead."[20]

But here Aristotle wants to make some distinctions. For instance, fearlessness in facing the prospect of death by drowning, disease, or accident are not occasions in which a man exhibits true fortitude. Why not? Because for Aristotle, they are not occasions worthy or "noble" enough to merit the name. We come, then, to his definition: "Fortitude is the virtue of the man who, being confronted with a noble occasion of encountering the danger of death, meets it fearlessly."[21]

Fortitude for Aristotle involves a "test" in which the person confronts some danger while engaged in a noble pursuit and either defends himself valiantly or dies in a dignified, heroic way. The key word throughout his discussion is "noble." The cause for which the person faces death must be a worthy one. It must be a cause greater than one's own selfish motives.

For Aristotle, there is really only one circumstance that fits this criteria; as he sees it, only "the perils of war answer this description most fully."[22] In Aristotle we find an understanding of the virtue that will continue throughout antiquity, even into our own day.

> What kind of death, then, does bring out courage? Doubtless the noblest kind, and that is death in battle. For in battle a man is faced by the greatest and most noble of dangers. This is corroborated by the honors which states, as well as monarchs, bestow upon courage.[23]

While the soldier is his model for the brave man, it is the cause for which the soldier fights that makes his bravery virtuous in Aristotle's account. Philip Ivanhoe, a scholar of comparative ethics, has explained: "Aristotle did recognize that the 'military courage' of professional soldiers — which relies solely on confidence in their soldierly skills — is only a semblance of real courage. Nevertheless, properly motivated and directed military courage — *martial courage directed toward ethically good ends — serves as his ideal.*"[24]

Fortitude, in this conception, is a public virtue related to patriotic goals and concerns for personal honor. And at the time of Christ, Aristotle's account of the virtue was the dominant view in the ancient world. The warrior, the soldier, was the model of the courageous man. Death for honor, for one's country, or for the common good becomes the epitome of fortitude. As Mary Louise Carlson, in a study of fortitude in classical and early Christian rhetoric, concluded: "This virtue was often associated especially with the defense of the state... a readiness to defy danger and to lay down one's life in battle."

Following Aristotle, classical writers often explained the virtue using military and patriotic examples — men who exhibited bravery on the battlefield or in defense of one's country. In the *Factorum et dictorum memorabilium libri novem* ("Memorable Sayings and Doings"), an influential early first-century collection on the virtues by Valerius Maximus, nearly every example cited in the fortitude chapter is from the battlefield.[25]

A favorite example in classical literature is that of Mucius Scaevola, a noble Roman youth whose fortitude earned him the respect of a foreign king he had tried to assassinate. The story, as told in Livy's *History of Rome,* is that around 500 B.C., the Etruscan King Porsena besieged Rome. Mucius was caught in Porsena's camp trying to kill the king. His defiant confession to his captor became famous: "I am your enemy, and as an enemy I would have slain you. I die as resolutely as I could kill: both to do and to endure valiantly [*et facere et pati fortia*] is the Roman way."[26]

Porsena was angry and ordered Mucius to be burned alive unless he revealed the names of his coconspirators. Mucius thrust his right hand into the flame to show his rejection of the king and his readiness to die. Livy reports that he allowed his hand to burn "as if his spirit were unconscious of sensation." This act of valor so impressed Porsena that he granted Mucius his freedom.[27]

We should note in this example something that recalls a point made in the previous chapter. Mucius's defiant reply about "the Roman way" is another classic example of the aggressive ideals of masculinity and manhood. "Willingness to endure pain and death was, indeed, central to the Roman idea of manliness," according to historian Myles McDonnell.[28]

There were other possibilities for the virtue of fortitude in the ancient world. The virtue is the subject of Plato's early dialogue, *Laches,* written about 390 years before Christ. In it, Socrates tries to help two generals who want to know how to teach courage and the other virtues to their children. Though many definitions of courage come up in the course of their conversation, no conclusion is reached about what courage actually is. But at one point, Socrates suggests a very wide-ranging profile for the virtue:

> I wanted to include not only those who are courageous in warfare but also those who are brave in dangers at sea, and the ones who show courage in illness and poverty and affairs of state; and then again I wanted not only those who are brave in the face of pain and fear but also those who are clever at fighting desire and pleasure, whether by standing their ground or running away.[29]

The tradition after Aristotle left these broader possibilities for fortitude behind. But with the rise of Stoicism, we see a return to Socrates' recognition of courage as self-discipline in the face of appetites, temptations, trials, and suffering. Thus, the statesman and philosopher Cicero could advise in 45 B.C.: "Take fortitude [*fortitudo* in Latin] for your guide, which will give you such a spirit that you will despise everything that can befall man, and look on it as a trifle."[30]

With Cicero we see an understanding of the virtue that is much broader than battlefield ethics. Certainly he endorses Aristotle's martial definition. For instance, in his *Tusculan Disputations,* he writes: "For what is fortitude except a disposition of the soul capable of endurance in facing danger and in toil and pain, as well as keeping all fear at a distance?"[31] But it is significant that Cicero also connects such heroic action with discipline and training aimed at self-mastery.

For Cicero, the soul who is wholly courageous (*omnino fortis*) has mastered his passions and is thereby able to achieve the Stoic end of remaining indifferent to whatever outward circumstances he finds himself in. And while Aristotle saw fortitude exercised mainly in pursuing honorable or patriotic goals, for Cicero the soul is most courageous when seeking the moral good. The wholly courageous person, he says, "cherishes the conviction that nothing but moral goodness and propriety deserves to be either admired or wished for or striven after, and that he ought not to be subject to any man or passion or any accident of fortune."[32]

As we will see, Christians assimilated this wider understanding of fortitude — as a form of discipline aimed at self-mastery in pursuit of the moral good. But to conclude our brief inquiry into how fortitude was understood at the time of Christ, let us turn to Seneca. A Roman rhetorician who was deeply influenced by Stoicism, Seneca was a contemporary of Jesus, born in 4 B.C. Seneca even has a family connection to New Testament history. His brother, Gallio, was the Roman proconsul who refused to hear the case brought by Jewish elders in Corinth against the apostle Paul.[33]

For Seneca, fortitude enables us to endure hardships patiently, especially those that threaten our lives. In one of his letters on moral and ethical concerns, he writes:

> Bravery [*fortitudo*] despises and challenges danger. The most beautiful and most admirable part of bravery is that it does not shrink from the stake, advances to meet wounds, and sometimes does not even avoid the spear, but meets it with opposing breast. If bravery is desirable, so is patient endurance of torture; for it is a part of bravery.... For it is not mere endurance of torture, but *brave* endurance, that is desirable. I therefore desire that "brave" endurance; and this is virtue.[34]

The Glory of Christian Fortitude

We can say, then, that for philosophers in the Roman Empire at the time of Christ, fortitude was the virtue of exalted manhood. It was an expression of a man's freedom, self-discipline, and interior and physical strength. Fortitude was that inner capacity that enabled him to resist natural enticements and to endure and make sacrifices in pursuit of goodness and justice. The virtue was a primary expression of Roman "manliness," and was closely related to aggressive physical strength and the ability to withstand pain in the context of military battle.

We can see a fierce individualism and a certain pride in human power and control underlying the Romans' ethical ideals. In Aristotle, for instance, the "man of virtue" seems to have as his "whole purpose... to live in such a way that he need not be forgiven anything. By giving favors rather than receiving them he insures his invulnerability to a love that might render him dependent."

These are the provocative words of Pinches and Hauerwaus.[35] And I think they are essentially right. The classical world could not come to a notion of infused virtues because it could not believe that God or the gods could be concerned and actively involved in people's lives. In fact, we can say that the Hellenistic ideal was based solely upon a supreme confidence in man's own powers. Moral progress was something the individual earned. The man proved his fortitude by his total independence — by demonstrating that he had no need for anybody else.

As Father Gauthier noted, for classical writers the particular function of fortitude was

> to assure man's autonomy in regard to the world. To accomplish this, there is only one way: teach man to find within man himself, that is to say, in his free will, the whole good of man... [I]n other words, [to] find the way to man's exaltation and an affirmation of his freedom in contempt for the world... finding within oneself the secret of one's happiness.[36]

With the coming of Christianity, fortitude was transformed. This is true of all the classical virtues. The Romans had long held up the virtue and heroism of select leaders as an example for others to follow. "Virtuous deeds implant in those who search them out a zeal and yearning that leads to imitation," wrote Plutarch at the introduction of his *Lives*.[37]

Christians could take this even farther — believing that the Author of all virtues, God himself, had come to dwell among us, that through the gift of his grace, people might live in "likeness to God." They believed that the power, the virtue of God, was "breathed" into believers by the Spirit at baptism, making them partakers of the divine nature and sons and daughters of God. In the lives of the saints and martyrs they saw confirmation that God empowered and strengthened those who believed in him.

Through their meditations on the beatitudes of Jesus, early Christian thinkers established a lofty new goal for the moral life. The ultimate happiness, the *summa bonum*, of the philosophers was to be communion with God, participation in his life. "We shall be like him," the early Christians believed.[38] The Christian was reborn in intimate friendship with God. And this intimacy makes all the difference in their approach to fortitude and the other virtues.

St. Ambrose modeled his book, *On the Duties of the Clergy*, on Cicero's *De officiis* [The Duties] and even used the same title and organizational structure. He adopts Cicero's Stoic understanding that the virtue is more than battlefield bravery. Fortitude, Ambrose agreed, involves self-control and the ability to restrain one's appetites, which are prerequisites to moral maturity and the formation of character.

> The glory of fortitude, therefore, does not rest only on
> the strength of one's body or of one's arms, but rather
> on the courage of the mind. Nor is the law of courage

exercised in causing, but in driving away all harm.... And in very truth, rightly is that called fortitude, when a man conquers himself, restrains his anger, yields and gives way to no allurements, is not put out by misfortunes, nor gets elated by good success, and does not get carried away by every varying change as by some chance wind. But what is more noble and splendid than to train the mind, keep down the flesh, and reduce it to subjection, so that it may obey commands, listen to reason, and in undergoing labors readily carry out the intention and wish of the mind.[39]

But as we read Ambrose's account, we immediately notice some striking differences from Cicero.[40] His authorities are sacred Scripture and the lives of the saints. He cites the bravery of biblical warriors such as Joshua, Samson, David, and Jude Maccabeus; he talks about the heroism of Daniel and the sufferings of Job and Eleazar. But his highest example of fortitude is that of the apostles and the martyrs, especially the deacon St. Lawrence and his holy bishop, Pope St. Sixtus II. We also see in Ambrose a radically new element — Jesus Christ as both model for Christian fortitude and the "strengthener" of those who suffer for the sake of his name.

We have to remember that Ambrose was writing for priests. And he held up St. Paul to priests as the example of "the true fortitude which Christ's warrior possesses." Paul, he said, "was strengthened in Christ Jesus, and ... though in dangers, in countless labors, in prisons, in deaths, he was not broken in spirit, but fought so as to become more powerful through his infirmities."[41]

The lesson for priests is that they must grow in the virtue of fortitude in which Christ strengthens them. Practice and growth in the virtue leads to "true freedom of the mind"[42] and a desire to put the pursuit of "all that is virtuous ... before anything else."[43] Those called to "duty in the Church," are called to work "so that Christ's power may show itself forth in us," Ambrose teaches. And to do this, the priest must imitate Christ in dying and rising to new life: "Let our flesh die, that in it every sin may die. And as though living again after death, may we rise to new works and a new life."[44]

With Ambrose, we are far beyond the classical understanding of the virtue. Although he adapted the thought of Cicero, Ambrose's account is radically shaped not only by the Gospel but by the experience of the Christian life. And we see this to varying degrees throughout the Church Fathers and other early Church writers.

In her extensive review of the literature, Carlson notices that writers such as Tertullian, Lactantius, Minucius Felix, Augustine, and Arnobius often made reference to the classical examples or *exempla* of Roman literature, along with references to biblical figures like Samson, David, Job, and Joshua, in writing about fortitude. She concludes:

> The Christians, despising motives of honor and praise, which they attributed to the Romans, devoted themselves to the principle that true glory is derived from God alone.... Thus the Church Fathers clearly placed a Christian stamp upon their definitions of fortitude. Nonetheless, they persisted in drawing upon the stock of pagan examples when urging Christians to courageous conduct.... If certain pagans were acknowledged to be courageous, surely the Christians, by being reminded of these models of fortitude, could be spurred with hopes of eternal reward to emulate and surpass their feats.[45]

For Christians facing the tortures of the emperor, certain Roman *exempla* came to acquire an ironic significance. Most often cited was the example we discussed above — that of

Mucius Scaevola. Why? Carlson suggests that it had to do with Mucius's endurance of the fire. "Perhaps bitter experience... caused this example to be fresh in the mind of Christians. Torture by fire... was a grim reality of the martyrs."[46]

Yet early Christian writers drew a bright line to separate their martyrs from examples of Romans glorified for killing themselves in the face of dishonor or unjust suffering. The Christians rejected any possibility that suicide could be an expression of fortitude. They believed that God was the Author of life and therefore that life belonged not to the individual but to God.

"Therefore," said Lactantius, a third-century apologist, "it is to be considered impious to wish to depart from it without the command of God. Therefore, violence must not be applied to nature."[47] That is what suicide was for the Christian then and now — a rejection of the gift of God, a violence against nature.

For the Christian, the courageous man cannot actively seek death or inflict it upon himself. Lactantius said that the Christian was the true witness to fortitude, because he was willing "to suffer torture and death rather than betray a trust or depart from his duty; or, overcome by fear of death or severity of pain, commit any injustice."[48]

Early Christian writers did, however, return to one figure in Roman history as if he were a kind of precursor to the courage of their martyrs. Almost as often as they cited Mucius, they referred to the celebrated story of Marcus Atilius Regulus, the Roman general who submitted to torture and execution at the hands of the Carthaginians during the First Punic War, about 250 years before Christ. According to the accounts of Cicero and Aulus Gelius, Regulus was forced to stand in a narrow box driven through with nails. The box fit so tightly around his body that if he leaned in any direction he would be pierced through. His captors held him this way until he died of sleep deprivation.

Some apologists saw in this an image of the crucifixion. "He was crammed into a sort of chest and everywhere pierced by nails driven in from the outside, he endured so many crucifixions (*tot cruces sensit*)," wrote Tertullian in his essay on the martyrs.[49] Augustine, too, sought to turn the example of Regulus to Christian ends. In a long discussion in *The City of God*, he holds the general up as "a very noble example of the voluntary endurance of captivity in obedience to a religious scruple."[50]

Augustine also used the example of Regulus to encourage Christians to reject the temptation of suicide and endure their sufferings with fortitude, confident in God's care.

> Having such a contempt of life, and preferring to end it by whatever torments excited enemies might contrive rather than terminate it by his own hand, [Regulus] could not more distinctly have declared how great a crime he judged suicide to be. Among all their famous and remarkable citizens, the Romans have no better man to boast of than this....
>
> But if the bravest and most renowned heroes, who had but an earthly country to defend... shrank from putting an end to their own lives even when conquered by their enemies; if, though they had no fear at all of death, they would yet rather suffer slavery than commit suicide, how much rather must Christians, the worshippers of the true God, the aspirants to a heavenly citizenship, shrink from this act, if in God's providence they have been for a season delivered into the hands of their enemies to prove or to correct them! And certainly, Christians subjected to this humiliating condition will not be deserted by the Most High, who for their sakes humbled himself.[51]

In this quotation, we see the main outlines of the Christian "difference" concerning fortitude. For the Romans the virtue was bound up with warfare, patriotism, and the love of honor. The early Church reoriented the virtue to the noble pursuit of the glory of heaven and the Kingdom of God, with joyful certainty that they would "not be deserted by the Most High, who for their sakes humbled himself." Fortitude for the Christian was a training, a proving, a discipline of the mind and the will, much as it was for the later Stoics.

Yet Christian fortitude was more than a spiritualized Stoicism. If Pieper rightly described fortitude as readiness to fall in battle, the Christian expanded the notion of the battlefield to include everywhere from the human heart to the tribunals, jails, and execution arenas of the tyrannical emperors.

Thus, Pope St. Gregory the Great took an expansive view of the virtue: "The courage of the just consists in conquering the flesh, in opposing the pleasures to which it is prone, in suppressing attachment to the pleasures of this life."[52] Augustine, too, saw fortitude as an essential virtue in the Christian's pursuit of wisdom and holiness: "It is a sign of fortitude to cut oneself adrift from all the deadly pleasures of the passing show and to fix his affection on things eternal."[53]

Christ was seen as the new exemplar of every virtue, as Ambrose affirmed: "The Master of obedience teaches us by his example concerning the precepts of virtue."[54] And all virtue was a reflection of the response of love that animated the Christian soul. Fortitude is the divine gift that enables us "to love the trials of this life for the sake of an eternal reward," said Gregory.[55] Again we could quote Augustine: "I hold virtue to be nothing else than perfect love of God.... Fortitude is love bearing everything readily for the sake of God."[56]

Be Strong and Have Courage!

This bearing of everything *for the sake of God* represents what I have been calling the radical newness of Christian fortitude.

The Romans celebrated the moral resolve and strength of those who died for honor or the noble cause of their country. They also celebrated those, like Regulus, who faced torture rather than betray an oath he had sworn by the Roman gods. But there was no equivalent, no precedent for the Christian belief that God is both the Author and the reason for the practice of the virtues.

The Christians taught that God himself gave the believer the fortitude that enabled him to persevere. This was something new in the history of world religions — although, as we see in the next chapter, this belief was anticipated and prepared for in the Jewish Scriptures. We hear this new dimension of fortitude in many of the stories of the martyrs. The tales of the martyrs were written, and read, as stories of virtue to be imitated.[57]

In his *Martyrs of Palestine*, Eusebius tells of Romanus, a young deacon at Antioch. Describing how the emperor ordered his tongue to be cut out, Eusebius observes: "But he endured this with fortitude and showed to all by his deeds that the power of God is present with those who endure any hardship whatever for the sake of religion, lightening their sufferings and strengthening their zeal."[58]

This is a beautiful statement of the promise of Christian fortitude. Fortitude is the power of God available to all who believe and serve him, enabling us to endure any hardship, giving us relief in our trials, strengthening our devotion. In these early writings, we always hear echoes of St. Paul — that our strength is not our own. The *Decretum Gelasianum*, the decree attributed to Pope Gelasius I (492–496), cites this as one of the reasons for meditating on the lives of the martyrs.

> [F]or edification ... the holy Roman Church, after the books of the Old and New Testaments, [permits the public reading of] the deeds of the holy martyrs, who are glorious from the manifold tortures they endured and their

wonderful triumphs of steadfastness. For what Catholic can doubt that they suffered more than is possible for human beings to bear, and did not endure this by their own strength, but by the grace and help of God.[59]

What was the source of their confident endurance? We have alluded to it before and explore it in greater detail in the chapters ahead. Christian fortitude is something radically new because at the heart of the faith is a brand-new understanding of death — a certainty that Jesus Christ, by dying on the cross and rising, has destroyed the power of death, hence delivering "all those who through fear of death were subject to lifelong bondage."[60]

This was the power of the cross that Paul spoke of — foolishness, as we have seen, to those who cannot believe in it. But for those who can, it is the very power of God for salvation.[61] The cross was the sign that death, the last enemy, had been defeated.[62] Because death was no longer the inevitable end of every human life, it was no longer anything to be afraid of.

The fear of death no longer held the Christians in bondage. This made the Christians fearless in rejecting the injustice and immorality of their society, in serving the poor and the sick, in bearing witness to their faith before judges, emperors, and executioners.

Thus, Tertullian, writing in the late second century, could reject the criticism of those who, like Epictetus and Marcus Aurelius, charged Christians with "obstinacy," not true courage. "All our obstinacy is . . . based on our strong conviction," he said. "For we take for granted a resurrection of the dead. Hope in this resurrection amounts to a contempt of death."[63] Because they trusted in the resurrection, they could embrace the cross of Christ. Because they trusted in the resurrection, they could give their lives as Christ had given his, confident that from their sacrifice they would be born into eternal life.

Nowhere was this identification with the sacrifice of Christ more apparent than in the early martyrdoms of priests. This is fitting because then, as now, the priest is the man of the Eucharist, acting in the person of Christ (*in persona Christi*) in offering the sacrifice of his Body and Blood. And the early martyrdoms of priests and bishops are told often in the language of the liturgy of sacrifice, in the language of the eucharistic celebration.[64]

Pope Benedict XVI has observed how the bishop Polycarp's martyrdom "is depicted as liturgy — indeed, as the process of the martyr's becoming a Eucharist, as he enters into full fellowship with the *Pascha* of Jesus Christ and thus becomes a Eucharist with him."[65] Polycarp described himself as a lamb offered as an oblation to, God and his final words took the form of a long eucharistic prayer in which he invoked the "eternal and celestial high priest, Jesus Christ."

The holy priest made a prayerful appeal in liturgical language, describing himself as the sacrificial offering: "May I be received this day… as a rich and acceptable sacrifice." At the "Amen" of Polycarp's prayer, the executioner lit the fire. But the crowd smelled, not burning flesh, but the sweet aroma of baked bread.

What intrigues me about this account also is this detail — that the crowd heard a voice from heaven as Polycarp entered the Roman amphitheatre: "Be strong [Greek: *ischue*], Polycarp, and have courage [*andrizou*]!"[66] Polycarp's entire trial unfolds under the divine promise of strength and fortitude. It underscores the early Christian confidence that the martyrs' ability to present their bodies as a living sacrifice[67] was dependent upon on the divine gift of fortitude — pledged and delivered from on high.

The priest's intimate relationship to Christ's sacrificial self-offering is again shown in the moving story of Pionius, a priest from Smyrna, Greece, martyred during the persecution of Decius. His courageous confession, made just before he was ordered hung by his fingernails, should be remembered by all of us who are called to Holy Orders: "I am a priest of the Catholic Church [*tēs katholikēs ekklēsias eimi presbyteros*]."[68] What a noble calling, to share in the sacrifice of Christ!

Later in his torture, as Pionius was being nailed to the gallows to be burned alive, he made what we can only describe as a eucharistic offering of his body to God. As reported in the ancient account, Pionius "looking up to heaven [*anablepsas de eis ton ouranon*], gave thanks [*eucharistēsas*] to God who had preserved him so; then he stretched himself out on the gibbet and allowed the soldier to hammer in the nails."[69]

It is moving to contemplate the literal echoes of our Lord's sacrifice — how he lifted his eyes to heaven and gave thanks before multiplying the loaves and fishes, and again before offering his Body and Blood in the Eucharist; how he stretched out his arms to be nailed to the gibbet of the cross.

So too today does the ministry of the priest depend on that gift of fortitude. *Be strong and have courage!* Only the gift of fortitude enables the priest, like the martyrs, to join the offering of his life to Christ's sacrificial offering of his life on the cross and in the Eucharist. In the fortitude of the martyrs we have an inspirational glimpse of the meaning of the priestly vocation as service of God or Christ — *servus Dei* or *servus Christi*. This service is liturgical and sacrificial in the sense that the priest is empowered to offer the sacrifice of Christ, the Eucharist.

But *servus Dei* also describes an attitude towards life — how the priest is called to a fearless offering of his life in love for the sake of the Lord, joining himself to Christ's total gift of himself and thus becoming able to communicate the fruits of Christ's sacrifice in the sacraments.

In the next two chapters, we look at the wellsprings of this spirituality of the martyrs, which are to be found in the pages of the Word of God.

CHAPTER 4

The Lord Is My Strength

The Old Testament Witness to Fortitude

THE STORIES ABOUT Servant of God Emil Joseph Kapaun are almost legendary. There was the time when the driver of a jeep carrying wounded soldiers was shot and killed by a sniper. Father Kapaun grabbed the wheel and steered the vehicle to safety through streets filled with fire and exploding shells. Another time, he carried a wounded man on a stretcher more than ten miles to get him medical attention.

In his four months on the frontlines of the United States' war with Korea, Father Kapaun distinguished himself as heroic and wise, and a compassionate counselor to soldiers far from home. He offered the Holy Mass on the hood of a jeep, heard confessions in foxholes, helped bury the dead, and consoled the shell-shocked. When he was finally captured by the Chinese Communists and held for more than two hundred days in a brutal South Korean prison, he was a model of strength and courage for his fellow captives. This is the testimony of one of them:

> He made me fight to stay alive when dying was so simple; it was easier to die than live in those days.... Our communist captors ... didn't know quite how to handle the priest because he could not be scared, threatened, cajoled, or humiliated. On the contrary, they feared this man whom they couldn't break; they trembled at the control and influence he had with all the men. It worried them

that this man could be so powerful with just his mild manner and soft speech, where they resorted to screaming, threatening with all forms of sadistic torture... and still couldn't influence us like this man of God.[1]

Young Emil had felt the call of the priesthood early. Growing up in a bilingual home in Pilsen, Kansas, the child of Bohemian immigrants from the Czech Republic, he used to play Mass by a tree in his backyard. He was an avid fisherman and outdoorsman, and on summer breaks from seminary training, he came home to work the family's farm. But he refused to use gloves. "I want to feel some of the pain our Lord felt when he was nailed to the cross," he explained.

He had a great love for the Eucharist and a very high vision of the priesthood. Just before his ordination in 1940, he wrote to a cousin with enthusiasm and amazement:

Think what it means! To offer up the living Body and Blood of our Savior every day in Holy Mass. To absolve souls from sin in holy Confession and snatch them from the gates of hell. These and a hundred more duties and responsibilities make a person realize that the vocation to the priesthood is so sublime that the angels in heaven were not given the honor; no, not even the Blessed Mother who was never stained with sin — even she was not called to be a priest of God. And here I am called![2]

As a military chaplain who participated in the invasion of Korea, he continued to perform his priestly duties even when he was a prisoner of war. He heard confessions, gave spiritual direction, and led the praying of the rosary. He defended the faith during the daily Communist indoctrination sessions. During one session, he enraged his instructor by pointing out that the Chinese dictator, Mao Tse-Tung — as powerful as he was — could never create a tree or a flower, as God was able to do.

Father Kapaun's leg became infected, and in the days following Easter in 1951, the pain became unbearable. He still insisted on hearing confessions. And he encouraged a group gathered around his bed by telling the story of the seven Maccabees, the courageous Jews who went to their deaths rather than obey the idolatrous commands of a foreign king. He spoke of the mother of the seven, and how she wept with joy during the torture of her sons, confident that they were going to God.

"As you see," he said, "I am crying too. Not tears of pain but tears of joy, because I'll be with my God in a short time."[3] After that, his captors took him to a so-called hospital that the Americans called the "death house" because so few came back from it alive. His friends believe the Communists finally killed Father Kapaun there.

Father Kapaun was an American priest of great fortitude who may one day be declared a saint. For me, it is inspiring and instructive that, in his final moments, this courageous priest was contemplating the Maccabees, the first martyrs for the God of Israel to be depicted in the pages of sacred Scripture. The story of the seven brothers and their heroic mother marks the climax of the Old Testament's witness to fortitude, and it is a very important episode for understanding later Christian development of the virtue.

There Is No Virtue of Fortitude in the Bible

The biblical books of Maccabees were written in Greek and show some of the vocabulary and influence of the Greek philosophical tradition that we looked at in the previous chapter. And, as we see near the end of this chapter, the book reflects an important stage in the encounter between biblical faith and the wider traditions of the Hellenistic world.

But what strikes us at first when we turn to the Bible is how remote it seems from that wider tradition. In fact, what strikes us is the virtual absence of any concept of fortitude and the other virtues, as those virtues were conceived in the Greco-Roman world. Father A. Gauthier, the Dominican theologian, goes so far as to say: "There is no virtue of fortitude in the Bible."[4] What he means is that when we enter into the sacred Scriptures, we enter a very different moral world.

That is not to say that the Bible has no concept of fortitude. Father Gauthier is quick to point that out. I think we can detect a kind of "pedagogy" of the virtue running through the pages of the Old and New Testaments. But the ways and means of biblical fortitude are much different than those we have identified in Greek and Roman philosophy and literature. As we will see, questions of human excellence, courage, and strength look much different through a biblical lens.

We can begin our study of the virtue at the end of the Jewish Bible. In 2 Chronicles 26, we read of King Uzziah of Judah, who reigned sometime in the middle of the eighth century before Christ. Uzziah was 16 when he succeeded his father Amaziah to the throne, and he set out to be a righteous king who would lead his people in the service of God. He received spiritual direction from the holy prophet Zechariah, and he resolved to "seek God," which is a sort of technical term in Chronicles for doing the will of God.

"And as long as he sought the LORD, God made him prosper," according to the biblical account. His army defeated the Philistines, and the kingdom grew and thrived, economically and militarily. Other nations came to pay tribute and to seek alliances with him. The biblical narrative stresses Uzziah's growing power. He "became very strong." He "fortified" the towers in Jerusalem. He mustered a massive army made up of "mighty men of valor" capable of "making war with mighty power."

But after a glowing report of his achievements, the author of Chronicles sounds an ominous note: "And his fame spread far, for he was marvelously helped, *till he was strong*." The point is immediately underlined: "But when he was strong he grew proud, to his destruction."

What happened to Uzziah is not as important to us as *why*. What brought about his downfall? The answer is in that ominous phrase: "till he was strong." When he was dedicated to seeking the Lord and serving his will, Uzziah was "marvelously helped." But then he became "strong." And in his strength, he forgot where he came from and how he got there. He forgot the true source of his earthly power and glory. He fooled himself into thinking that what he had accomplished was solely of his own doing. And this became his undoing.

When he was strong he grew proud. This could serve as an epitaph not only for Uzziah, but for many figures in the Old Testament. It is a pattern we find throughout the Bible. And it is the gateway for us to enter into and reflect on the biblical idea of fortitude.

We immediately sense the difference between the biblical and classical understandings. They almost seem like mirror opposites. If for the Greeks and Romans, man is the measure of the virtue, the starting point for the Bible is God. Fortitude in the Bible is not a virtue that is acquired by developing inner strength and the ability to bravely defend one's honor or nation.

For the biblical authors, fortitude is a means for achieving the interior freedom needed to detach from worldly concerns, especially the fear of death, in order to serve God and the law of his kingdom. This is why Father Gauthier can say there is no virtue of fortitude in the Bible. The Bible talks, not of human fortitude and virtue, but of the creative and redemptive power of God — and of how we can share, as his sons and daughters, in God's power and promises.

Let Not the Mighty Man Glory in His Might

The Greeks and Romans focused on human strength and power. The Old Testament treats these human attributes as illusions. Kings are not saved by their armies, nor are men who seem strong saved by their strength. "Let not the mighty man glory in his might... but let him who glories glory in this — that he understands and knows me, that I am the LORD."[5] This summarizes the whole biblical witness on human power and strength.

As we see from the example of Uzziah, success, victory, and the accumulation of earthly power are occasions of temptation, sin, and doom. Throughout the Old Testament, pride and strength are two sides of the same bad coin. The holy monk, St. John Cassian, writing in the fifth century, uses Uzziah as a cautionary tale.

> From this you may understand how dangerous success in favorable affairs can be — so much so that those who could not be broken by adversity are all the more harshly crushed by prosperity if they are heedless, and those who have come through crises, who were in conflict or on the verge of death, succumb to their own victories and triumphs.[6]

These are wise words, especially for the man who would be a priest. By definition, the priest is ordained to serve God, as Uzziah was anointed king to serve God. But success — even in the service of God (what Cassian calls "favorable affairs") — can be dangerous to our spiritual lives.

It is not simply material wealth that Cassian and the Scriptures speak of. The warning can apply to such things as the successful accomplishments of our pastoral plans and priorities.

We can become too impressed with ourselves, enamored of the little trophies and triumphs of our work. We need to watch out for this. It can lead us to make errors of judgment. Over time, the habits of pride can weaken us, rendering us unable to face struggles and adversity. In the worst cases, pride can become our undoing, as it was for Uzziah.

There is a certain realism involved here in recognizing that everything we have we have received from God who is the giver of every good gift.[7] The philosopher-priest, Blessed Antonio Rosmini, used to say that the danger comes "when we forget what we continually receive from God and attribute it to ourselves — when we trust in our own powers, our own skills, our knowledge, our strength."[8]

Reading the Old Testament should be a bracing corrective to the pride and vainglory that may accompany our success. For instance, in Isaiah, we read: "[God] will punish the arrogant boasting of the king... and his haughty pride. For he [the king] says: 'By the strength of my hand I have done it.'"[9]

In the prophet Ezekiel's lament over the King of Tyre, the king's pride and self-sufficiency is defined as a kind of self worship.

> Your heart is proud and you have said, "I am a god"...
> yet you are but a man, and no god,
> though you consider yourself as wise as a god.[10]

Ezekiel fills his prophetic testimony with images that compare Tyre's king to the first man, Adam. The king is described as having been created in Eden, the "garden of God," and mention is made of the same precious stones found in Eden. The King, like Adam, is said to have fallen from grace by wanting to be like God.[11]

One interpretation is that the prophet wants us to understand pride as the primal human sin, and a deadly one at that.

In our pride we forget God and think that what we have we have gained by our own power and cleverness. That is what happened to the King of Tyre, according to the prophet — his heart swelled with pride as the gold and silver in his treasuries increased.[12]

This is a common biblical theme. Moses, too, strikes this note in his long homily about Israel's years of testing and purification in the wilderness:

> Beware lest you say in your heart, "My power and the might of my hand have gotten me this wealth." You shall remember the LORD your God. For it is he who gives you power to get wealth, *that he may confirm his covenant*.[13]

I underline that last point. God is the source of all power and strength. But there is an order and a purpose to all that God does. And the gift of his power is given, as Moses points out, to *confirm his covenant* — that is, to fulfill the purposes of his covenant plan. This is especially important for priests to understand, because the priesthood, the "ordained ministry of the new covenant,"[14] is at the center of God's covenant plan. God does not give his priests power for power's sake or for our own sake — but for the sake of the economy of salvation, his covenant plan for humanity and history.

Covenant and the Kingdom of Priests

We need to make a brief excursus. To fully understand the biblical virtue of fortitude as it relates to the priesthood, it is important to understand the covenant relationship that God seeks to establish with his people. This is a vast topic, of course, but we need to have at least a shared set of working assumptions.

God is "the God of the covenant," who "comes to meet man by his covenants."[15] The history of the world is the unfolding of God's covenant purposes. Through the series of covenants he makes, beginning with his covenant with Abraham and continuing through the new covenant of Jesus Christ, God is fulfilling his purposes for creation — to bless the people he created with his presence and life; to dwell with them as a Father, and "to gather into one the children of God who are scattered abroad" in every nation.[16]

In his covenant plan, God established Israel as "a kingdom of priests and a holy nation."[17] What that meant is that Israel would be a light to the nations, causing the teaching of the living God to go out to the ends of the earth. Jesus was sent from God to make a new and everlasting covenant that established his Church as the fulfillment of Israel's identity and mission. The Church is the "Israel of God,"[18] and by the new covenant is "a chosen race, a royal priesthood, a holy nation."[19]

What does it mean for the Church to be a kingdom of priests? It means that all believers participate in Christ's mission, spreading the good news of the Kingdom of God and the forgiveness of sins to the ends of the earth. In that kingdom, the ordained priesthood plays an irreplaceable role. Under the old covenant, God called the tribe of Levi to serve him as priests — to teach and to lead the people, and to offer gifts and sacrifices for their sins.[20] In the kingdom of priests, it was the essence of the Levitical priesthood to "keep the people aware of its priestly character and to work so that it might live in accordance with it, so that it might glorify God with its entire existence."[21]

The unique characteristic of Levi was that the tribe was not alloted its own portion of the Promised Land.[22] God alone was to be the "ground" of the priestly existence. This is why in earlier generations, the priestly ordination ceremony included the verse from the Psalter: "The LORD is my chosen portion and my cup; you hold my lot."[23]

As Pope Benedict has said, this has a precise meaning for the priesthood today: "The true foundation of the priest's life, the ground of his existence, the ground of his life, is God himself....The priest can and must also say today, with the Levite: *Dominus pars hereditatis meae et calicis mei.* God himself is my portion of land — the external and internal foundation of my existence.[24]

The Catholic priesthood grows out of the Old Testament priesthood, which was prefigured by the priesthood of Jesus Christ, "the one mediator between God and men."[25] As we discuss more in the next chapter, when St. Mark describes Jesus' appointment of the apostles, he uses a Greek term associated in the Old Testament with priestly ordination. Jesus is said, literally, to have "*made* twelve."[26] This is priestly ordination langugage. And at the Last Supper he definitively "institutes his apostles as priests of the new covenant."[27]

The Church's sacramental liturgy, presided over by the priest in the person of Christ (*in persona Christi*), marks the final fulfillment of God's covenant plan. God had promised to bless all the families of the earth through the children of Abraham. This promise is fulfilled in the liturgy of the Church, in which the baptized are made sons and daughters of God and children of Abraham.[28] In the beautiful words of the *Catechism:*

> From the beginning until the end of time the whole of God's work is a blessing. From the liturgical poem of the first creation to the canticles of the heavenly Jerusalem, the inspired authors proclaim the plan of salvation as one vast divine blessing.... In the Church's liturgy the divine blessing is fully revealed and communicated. The Father is acknowledged and adored as the source and the end of all the blessings of creation and salvation.[29]

All of the gifts and virtues given to the priest, including the gift and virtue of fortitude, assist him in his sacred role of mediating the Father's blessings to his children. To adapt the words of Moses, God gives the priest his powers and his virtues in order to confirm his covenant plan.[30]

But we should not forget Moses' warning. We must be wary of the snare of pride. This is the lesson that earlier we saw Father Ciszek learning in the Lubianka prison camp. It is ultimately a lesson about the true source of our strength and power. Without God, we have no real strength, despite what we might be tempted to believe. We need to recognize that God alone is powerful and that our efforts will be effective only to the extent that we tap into that source of divine power.

Seeking the Lord and His Strength

If the first lesson of the Old Testament's pedagogy on fortitude is that human strength is an illusion, the second is a natural corollary. It is that God alone possesses strength and power in this world. The God of the Bible is the God of the Creed — "the Father Almighty, Creator of heaven and earth, and of all that is seen and unseen." By his strength he establishes the mountains.[31] By the strength of his "hand" or his "mighty arm" he delivers his people from bondage.[32] He is the "Mighty One" of Israel.[33] In the great psalm that he composed to celebrate the installation of the Ark of the Covenant in Jerusalem, David sings: "Seek the LORD and his strength!"[34]

Seek the Lord and his strength! This must be the pledge and mission of every priest. The priest must be a man who seeks the Lord and his strength, and who knows that his own strength can only be found in the Lord. Seeking God means trusting in his power, mercy, and love. The short verses below reflect this deep theme of Old Testament faith. In fact, these verses would make good pious aspirations for the priest to say throughout the day to bolster his growth in fortitude.

He gives power to the faint…
They who wait on the LORD shall renew their strength.[35]

Wait for the LORD;
be strong, and let your heart take courage.[36]

Be strong and let your heart take courage,
all you who wait for the LORD![37]

The LORD is my rock, and my fortress, and my
    deliverer....
my shield and the horn of my salvation, my
    stronghold....
who girded me with strength and made my way safe.[38]

We find aspirations like these throughout the psalms. It is no coincidence that the psalms make up the bulk of our daily prayer as priests in the Liturgy of the Hours. The psalms are the songs of the man who seeks the Lord and trusts in him as his rock and stronghold. As priests, we should always pray the Liturgy of the Hours as men seeking the Lord and seeking to grow in the virtues, especially fortitude.

As the psalmists did, we need to ask for the strength to abandon ourselves to his will, and to serve his covenant plan. Seeking God, in the sense that the Bible understands it, is always an act of faith, an act of self-abandonment to his providence and care. Yet humbly entrusting ourselves to God requires that we face up to our natural fears and set aside our instinctive self-protections.

The prayers for courage and strength that we hear in the psalms and prophets are founded on trust in God's Word. The act of faith heard most often — "the LORD is my strength" — first appears in the Old Testament canon in the ancient victory song the Israelites sang upon their deliverance from Egypt.[39]

In the Old Testament imagination, the Exodus is the "proof" that God will always remember his covenant promise to Abraham.[40] Because God is true to his Word, and because he proved faithful to Israel in the Exodus, the Israelites could be confident that he would always act in their history and in the lives of every believer. They could be assured that no matter what suffering might befall them, God would give them the strength they need to endure and to serve him. This hope runs through the Old Testament:

> Ascribe power to God... the God of Israel.
> He gives power and strength to his people.[41]

Be Strong and of Good Courage

This brings us to another component of Old Testament fortitude — the belief in God's saving presence and help. In our last chapter, we saw the early martyrs' trust — that God was truly with them, strengthening them in their trials. Their strength and hope originates in the biblical faith of Israel.

Be strong and be of good courage. That was the refrain of Moses' speech to Israel as he handed the nation's leadership over to Joshua. It was late in the book of Deuteronomy and Israel was on the threshold of the Promised Land. Moses, at age 120, had been told by God that he would not cross over the Jordan with his people. Instead, Joshua would lead them into the land.[42] Moses wanted to give the people the courage to go on. He told them:

> Be strong and of good courage! Do not fear.... It is the LORD who goes before you; *he will be with you*, he will not fail you or forsake you; do not be dismayed.[43]

Later, God himself makes the same promise to Joshua:

> Be strong and of good courage; be not frightened, neither be dismayed; for *the LORD your God is with you* wherever you go.[44]

To be strong and of good courage is perhaps one of the best definitions of what fortitude means in the Old Testament. It is a power and strength that comes as the pure gift of God's own presence. The gift of fortitude, as we see it in the Old Testament, must be received in an attitude of self-abandonment, rooted in trust in God's power and his faithfulness to his covenant.

This is beautifully expressed in King David's final instructions to his son, Solomon. David, of course, was talking about the task entrusted to Solomon of building the Temple at Jerusalem. But his words apply as well to each of us who seeks to be a servant of God's covenant will:

> *Be strong and of good courage*, and do it. *Fear not*, be not dismayed; for the LORD God, even my *God, is with you.* He will not fail you or forsake you, until all the work for the service of... the LORD is finished.[45]

By My God I Can Leap Over a Wall

As we saw in the previous chapter, the Romans had numerous historical *exempla* of the virtue of fortitude, and Christians could find many models of strength and courage in the Old Testament. Several of Israel's heroes — Joshua, Gideon, Samson, and David — well fit the warrior profile that epitomized the Roman ideal of fortitude.

Already within the New Testament, we see the figure of Job being held up as a model of steadfast and patient endurance in the face of sufferings due to the faith. This reflects a new type of courageous witness — the virtuous man who suffers injustice patiently for the sake of his faith in the true God. St. James extolled "the steadfastness of Job," who lost his loved ones, all his wealth and possessions, and even his health, but remained faithful to God.[46]

The Fathers of the Church go on to describe Job as a model of fortitude in the face of tests and challenges to the faith.[47] St. Gregory the Great, for instance, said that Job teaches us "to exhibit patience in the midst of trials."[48] In these early interpretations of Job, we see the marks of what I have called "the radical newness" of Christian fortitude when compared with how the virtue was understood in the Greek and Roman world.

As the Jesuit biblical scholar Cardinal Jean Daniélou said, Job's patience was "*not* a question of Stoical patience, of pure resignation bearing witness to greatness of soul. It is *patience linked with hope, founded on the certainty of the happiness promised by Christ*; and this certainty gives strength to endure the trials of earthly life."[49]

This new type of courage seems to grow naturally from the soil of the Old Testament beliefs we have been examining up to this point. There emerges as we progress through the Old Testament a bold new spirituality of courage and self-sacrifice. We see it especially in the prophets and the wisdom literature. But we even begin to notice in the later historical books a new "consciousness," a recognition that Israel's ritual sacrifices are not enough — that each believer must make his own life a sacrificial offering of praise and thanksgiving.

"Will the LORD be pleased with thousands of rams?" No, the prophet Micah replies. God desires not animal sacrifices, but works of justice and mercy.[50] The psalmist too reaches the same conclusion: "Sacrifice and offering thou dost not desire, but [rather]... delight to do thy will, O my God."[51]

This attitude will be fully developed in the preaching of Christ[52] and in St. Paul's beautiful teachings about spiritual worship,[53] which form a part of the Eucharistic Prayer of the Church. It is beyond my purposes to go much deeper into the subject here. My point is this: we begin to find in the Old Testament a strong connection between a spirituality of self-offering and a belief that God strengthens the faithful when they are facing enemies or other threats to their lives.

For example, in Psalm 50, we hear:

Offer to God a sacrifice of thanksgiving....
and call upon me in the day of trouble;
I will deliver you and you shall glorify me....
He who brings thanksgiving as his sacrifice honors me;
to him ... I will show the salvation of God.[54]

The Hebrew word translated "thanksgiving" in the above passage is *tōdāh*. Scholars have long identified certain psalms, such as Psalm 50, as the "*tōdāh* psalms" — psalms likely composed to accompany the offering of thanksgiving sacrifices in the Temple.[55] These psalms provide us a window into the development of the biblical notion of fortitude.

The *tōdāh* psalms follow a basic pattern. First, the singer describes a life-threatening danger he encountered or an affliction he suffered. Then he professes his faith in God and his confidence that God will deliver him. Finally, the psalm concludes with a hymn of thanksgiving, as the singer thanks God for saving him and giving him the strength to endure his hour of trial.

Psalm 18 is a classic *tōdāh* psalm. The singer professes himself to be a faithful servant of God, keeping all his commandments.[56] He describes his deep suffering. His enemies, men of violence, had him surrounded,[57] and his death seemed certain.[58] He called to the Lord in his distress, and the Lord heard his cry.[59] God did even more than deliver him from death.[60] God gave him the power to endure and to overcome his strife. God girded him with strength,[61] and by God's might he was able to subdue his enemies.

The psalmist gives us this vivid picture of the courage God gave him:

Yea, thou dost light my lamp;
The LORD my God lightens my darkness,
Yea, by thee I can crush a troop,
and by my God I can leap over a wall.[62]

Psalm 18, and the *tōdāh* psalms in general, are beautiful expressions of the later development of the biblical virtue of fortitude. In these psalms we see a new spirituality emerging, one in which the outward signs of worship — sacrifice and prayer — are joined to a new "interior" attitude of self-sacrifice. As the German theologian Hartmut Gese has said, in the *tōdāh* spirituality, "there developed a new, inward understanding of suffering... and in addition, the external sacrifice of thanksgiving is transformed into an inward sacrifice of one's own life."[63]

Scholars like Gese and Pope Benedict believe that the *tōdāh* is one of the sources of the Eucharist.[64] This is fascinating but unfortunately beyond what I can take up in this book. For our purposes we want to acknowledge the beginnings of this new spirituality in the Old Testament canon and to observe that this new understanding of suffering and interior sacrifice is based on Israel's belief that divine strength is available to those who believe in the Lord's promise of salvation and who humbly submit themselves to the divine will.

To Suffer Wrong Rather Than Do Wrong

From this kind of courage it is a short leap to the patient endurance of suffering for God's sake. The idea of patient suffering and holy martyrdom forms a bridge to the New Testament teaching on fortitude, which we take up in the next chapter. To move across that bridge, we turn first to the book of Daniel.

The tale told in Daniel 3 describes events presumed to have taken place in the sixth century before Christ, when Israel was exiled in Babylon under the harsh rule of King Nebuchadnezzar. In the writings of the early Christians, this is a story *par excellence* of courage and piety in the service of the living God.

Nebuchadnezzar had made a golden idol of himself and commanded that all his subjects fall down and worship it at regularly appointed hours. Three young Israelites — Shadrach, Meschach, and Abednego — refused. They calmly defended their beliefs to the king, including their belief that God has the power to deliver them from evil and death.[65]

Their testimony continued even after they were bound hand and foot and cast into the flames. They sang hymns praising God and imploring his strength and protection. They appealed to God's covenant, and his "marvelous works" of deliverance in the past.[66] And as the story continued, God strengthened them and protected them — by providing his very presence. One "like a son of the gods"[67] appeared in the furnace with the three brave young men. And the flames did not touch them.

The story concluded with the tyrant's "conversion," or at least a temporary change of heart. Nebuchadnezzar blessed "the God of Shadrach, Meschach, and Abednego — who has sent his angel and delivered his servants, who trusted in him... and yielded up their bodies rather than serve and worship any god except their own God."[68]

With these three servants of God, we see a new kind of biblical hero. They clearly have been well-formed in the Law of God. They know the letter of the Law, what God requires, and they are obedient to the Law. But they also know the spirit of the Law. Their love of God, the virtue upon which all the Law and prophets hinge, inspires their brave response to Nebuchadnezzar's unjust decree.

Because they trusted in God's power and his promises, they received the gift of his strength and courage. This gift enabled them to face pain, suffering, and death without fear. And God was "with them" in their trouble — in the form of the angelic "son" who came to them in the furnace.

What is new and remarkable is their willingness to "yield up their bodies" rather than commit sin or violate their covenant vows to God. Among the many Church Fathers to remark on this was St. Cyprian. "The strength of faith and valor is manifested in believing and knowing that God can deliver from immediate death and yet at the same time having no fear of death nor flinching from it and thereby proving one's faith all the more vigorously," he said.[69]

St. Augustine noticed this, too. He drew a connection between the fortitude of Daniel's threesome and St. Paul's mention of submitting to martyrdom by fire.[70] Again, as we saw in the last chapter, the man of courage does not commit an act of self-violence or self-mutilation; he chooses to submit to the violence of the persecutor instead of committing an act that would violate his conscience.

> Notice carefully and understand in what sense Scripture says that anyone should deliver his body to be burned. Not certainly, that he should jump into the fire when harassed by a pursuing enemy but that, *when a choice is offered him either of doing wrong or suffering wrong, he chooses not to do wrong rather than not to suffer wrong.* In this case, he delivers his body not to the power of the slayer, as those three men did who were being forced to adore the golden statue.... They refused to adore the idol, but they did not cast themselves into the fire.[71]

This is the beginning of a new biblical ethic of self-sacrifice and self-offering for the love of God. This ethic will be fully developed in the New Testament. And at the heart of this ethic is the virtue of fortitude, the gift of courage that God gives to them to carry out their heroic act of faith. We hear this expressed in the three boys' prayer:

> Yet with a contrite heart and a humble spirit may we be
>   accepted....
> Such may our sacrifice be in thy sight this day,
> and may we wholly follow thee,

for there will be no shame for those who trust in thee.
And now with all our heart we follow thee... and seek
  thy face....
Deliver us in accordance with thy marvelous works,
and give glory to thy name, O Lord.[72]

St. Ambrose viewed the boys' courage as a model for Christian fortitude, which he described in eloquent terms that merge Hellenistic ideals of the virtue with the biblical witness.

It falls to the one who has been perfected to sustain nature's common lot with courageous spirit, to bring it to better things and not to give way before those experiences that most people consider fearful and frightening. Instead, like a brave soldier, one must withstand onslaughts of the most severe calamities and undergo conflicts.... He is not weak in regard to wrongs done to his own or anxious about the burial of his body, for he knows that heaven is its due.... The one who is perfected is such that he wishes to do good to all people and desires that no evil befall anyone; but if something happens beyond his wish, he loses nothing of his own happiness.[73]

To Die a Good Death Willingly and Nobly

We conclude our review of the Old Testament by looking at a final dramatic example of fortitude — the stories of the holy martyrs told in 2 Maccabees. This was the story that was on Father Joseph Kapaun's mind in his final hours in the Communist prison camp. The story has been a source of inspiration to Christians from the beginning, and the Church's liturgy still presents their story to the faithful near the conclusion of the Church year.[74]

In many ways the books 1 and 2 Maccabees reflect the encounter of Jewish and Greek thought. The books were handed on to us in Greek and bear a Greek stamp. They tell the story of Israel's life under foreign occupation in the 150 or so years before Christ. In the 1 Maccabees portrait of Judas Maccabeus and his fellow revolutionaries, we see an almost classic portrayal of fortitude as a warrior virtue in the service of patriotic or nationalistic values. But, in 2 Maccabees we see a transformation — a move from "holy warfare" to "holy martyrdom."[75]

We want to look at the portraits of holy martyrdom — those Jews who chose to die rather than obey the anti-Jewish edicts of the occupying government. The scene is "harsh and utterly grievous."[76] King Antiochus IV had defiled the Jerusalem Temple and issued a series of laws that essentially forbade the practice of the Jewish religion. For the crime of circumcising their children, women were stripped and paraded around the city before being hurled to their deaths from the city walls along with their babies. Those caught observing the sabbath were burned alive.[77]

The persecution included using violence to force Jews to sacrifice pigs to pagan deities and then eat the pig-meat — idolatrous practices not allowed by the Law of Moses. 2 Maccabees gives us two stories of Jewish nonviolent resistance to these indignities — that of Eleazar, a 90-year-old scribe, and that of an anonymous mother and her seven sons.

Eleazar was tortured on the rack after refusing to eat the swine's flesh, while the mother and her sons were each tortured viciously and then killed. Throughout the accounts their actions are described with various Greek words associated with the virtue of fortitude, translated variously by such words as "courage," "courageously," and "manfully."[78]

There are many remarkable things about these stories, including a moving description by the mother of her faith in God as the Father of life in the womb.[79] But for our purposes, we want to notice these believers' readiness to face suffering and death as a consequence of their beliefs.

One of the seven sons says, "We are ready to die rather than transgress the laws of our fathers."[80] The elderly Eleazar says: "By manfully giving up my life now, I will... leave to the young a noble example of how to die a good death willingly and nobly for the revered and holy laws."[81] We also notice their faith and complete trust in God's covenant promises, expressed in an explicit hope that God would raise them from the dead.[82] As the youngest of the brothers and the last to die says: *"Our brothers, after enduring a brief suffering, have drunk of overflowing life under God's covenant."*

Let this be the last word of our Old Testament study. In the Maccabeean martyrs we see the full development of the Old Testament's teaching on fortitude. We see their faith in the "mighty power" of God[83] and their "whole trust" in him.[84]

Their trust in God's faithfulness to his covenant promises, their primitive hope in the resurrection, is the foundation of their courage. In their faith, these servants of God are given the courage and strength to endure the unendurable — to have their tongues cut out, their heads scalped, their bodies burned alive. Through it all, the gift of divine fortitude, accepted in the humility of those who know that God alone is their strength, enables them to testify to their persecutors of their faith in the Lord who made heaven and earth, and who holds all souls in his gaze.

CHAPTER 5

Be Not Afraid

The Power of Christ and the
Apostolic Priesthood

MY OWN PRIESTHOOD HAS BEEN deeply shaped by the teaching and witness of Pope John Paul II. I had been ordained only three months when he appeared in the window of the papal apartment in St. Peter's Square on October 22, 1978, and proclaimed those thrilling first words of his historic pontificate: "Be not afraid to welcome Christ and accept his power!"

And I was still a young priest when he paid a pastoral visit to San Antonio on September 13, 1987. That morning, I had the joy of concelebrating Mass for 350,000 faithful with the Vicar of Christ and other priests from San Antonio and across Texas. It is a day I will not forget as long as I live. In 2001, John Paul called me to be a bishop; and in 2005, shortly before his death, he called me to be an archbishop. I feel humbled and blessed. There are many nights I reflect upon the fact that the apartment that is now my home at Assumption Seminary was the place where this holy man and heroic leader spent the night praying and resting when he came to San Antonio.

As I have grown in my priesthood and episcopal ministry, John Paul has served as one of my primary role models. He was a man of prayer and action and a man of learning; he was compassionate and dedicated to holiness. Most of all, I admire his example of fortitude. From the sadness and hardship of losing his brother and his parents at a young age, to his endurance and daring under both Nazi and Soviet occupations, to his resistance to Communism during his papacy — his life was a profile in courage.

His own vocation was deeply influenced by those experiences, and by the witness of the thousands of Polish priests martyred by both the Nazis and Soviet regimes — many of whom he beatified or canonized while he was Pope. Late in his life, he wrote: "Their sacrifice on the altar of history helped to make my priestly vocation a reality.... [B]y their sacrifice they showed me the most profound and essential truth about the priesthood of Christ."[1]

Fearlessness and courage were the underlying spiritual and moral themes of his pontificate. Looking back, it now seems providential that his first public teachings were on the subject of the cardinal virtues. Less than a month after his election, on November 15, 1978, he gave a teaching on the virtue of fortitude. He issued this challenge:

> We need strong men! To be men we need fortitude. The truly prudent man, in fact, is only he who possesses the virtue of fortitude; just as also the truly just man is only he who has the virtue of fortitude. Let us pray for this gift of the Holy Spirit which is called the "gift of fortitude." When man lacks the strength to "transcend" himself in view of higher values — such as truth, justice, vocation, faithfulness in marriage — this "gift from above" must make each of us a strong man and, at the right moment, say to us deep down: *Courage!*[2]

John Paul was the pope of courage. He wanted to set men free, to make them strong and fearless in service to God and in their pursuit of supernatural values. His legacy will be forever captured in those first words: "Be not afraid!" For more than a quarter century he would teach us that Jesus Christ has conquered death and that the "power of Christ's cross and res-urrection is greater than any evil which man could or should fear."[3]

Fear of Death and the Bondage of Sin

John Paul's prophetic first words as Pope are taken straight from the heart of the Gospel. Literally from beginning to end, the Gospel is a divine call to fearlessness, to courage. "Be not afraid!" is the glad tiding the angel brings to Mary at the an-nunciation of Christ.[4] An angel uses the same words in pro-nouncing to the women at the tomb that Christ has risen from the dead. Jesus himself assures his apostles with these words, and the gospels record as his first words after the resurrection: "Be not afraid!"[5]

In the Old Testament, this was a common expression of di-vine assurance in the presence of God's angels or messengers.[6] But in the New Testament, it means much more than that. The angel's message to Mary — "Be not afraid, Mary, for you have found favor with God" — is meant for the whole human race. The coming of Christ means the days of fear have ended for the human race. By his life, death, and resurrection, Jesus strikes at the root of every fear — the fear of death.

As we have observed, the virtue of fortitude presumes that by nature we are aware of our own mortality and our vulner-ability to bodily harm. Fortitude is what helps us deal with our fear of getting hurt and our fear of the ultimate injury, death. We have quoted the great philosopher of the virtues, Joseph Pieper: "All fortitude stands in the presence of death. Fortitude is basically readiness to die or, more accurately, readiness to fall, to die, in battle."[7] And we have seen how Christian think-ers in the early centuries of the Church defined these "battle-fields" as interior as well as exterior — fortitude being essential for both spiritual warfare and military combat.

As we turn to study the New Testament witness, we see the roots of the Christian tradition's deep "interiorization" and "supernaturalization" of the virtue. Pieper sums up the Gospel witness well: "The virtue of fortitude keeps man from so loving his life that he loses it."[8] He is making an allusion to Jesus' words: "For whoever would save his life will lose it; and whoever loses his life for my sake, he will save it."[9]

When we are confronted in this way with the starkness of the Gospel, we are able to see clearly that fortitude — courage and fearlessness in the face of death — is at the heart of what Jesus expects of his disciples. More than that, the gift of this strength is at the heart of the good news he brings to us.

"Do not fear those who kill the body but cannot kill the soul; rather fear him who can destroy both soul and body in hell," Jesus said.[10] On one level, this is practical advice to people who are going to suffer persecution and torture for their belief in him. But it also reflects a radically new perspective on the meaning of life and death. The courage that Christ demands is at the same time a gift he bestows on those who believe in him.

Here we see the deep psychology of the Gospel at work. The fear of being wounded, the fear that we might be killed, inhibits us from doing good and from striving for the holiness and discipleship to which Christ calls us. We all know this from experience. Often we do not do what the Lord requires because we are afraid that it will get us into trouble, that it will "hurt" somehow — physically, mentally, emotionally. This fear is rooted in the reality of sin. St. Augustine explained it this way:

> Among all things which are possessed in this life, the body is, by God's most righteous laws, for the sin of old, man's heaviest bond.... Lest this bond should be shaken and disturbed, the soul is shaken with the fear of toil

and pain; lest it should be lost and destroyed, the soul is shaken with the fear of death. For the soul loves the body from the force of habit, not knowing that by using it well and wisely, its resurrection and reformation will, by the divine help and decree, be without any trouble made subject to its authority. But when the soul turns to God wholly in this love, it knows these things and so will not only disregard death, but will even desire it.[11]

Augustine teaches that man is created a creature of body and soul. As such, the soul's greatest possession is his own body. The soul is ultimately afraid of being hurt or separated from the body in death. This fear can debilitate the soul. As Augustine recognizes, this fear of injury and death is a consequence of original sin ("the sin of old"). Because of original sin, death came into the world, and the fear of pain and death became a part of the human condition. Yet, as Augustine also says, thanks to Christ's resurrection, the soul is able, by the grace of God and by keeping his commands, to conquer death and know the resurrection of the body.

The starting point for a Gospel-based fortitude lies in this understanding of Christ's saving work. We read in the book of Wisdom: "God created man for incorruption and made him in the image of his own eternity. But through the devil's envy death entered the world."[12] This ancient interpretation of the "fall" in Genesis 3 forms the basis for the Church's teachings about original sin. St. Paul said: "Sin came into the world through one man and death through sin, and so death spread to all men because all men sinned."[13]

With original sin, the preservation of life — staying alive and avoiding pain — becomes perhaps the highest natural good of human existence. Love of self is not simply moral selfishness or narcissism. It is rooted in the natural desire to safeguard the self from destruction. Self-preservation, even through cowardice, becomes an understandable strategy of life under the regime of sin and death. We fear not only physical injury, but other damage as well — to our reputations, our feelings, our sense of pride and self-esteem. All of these fears are rooted in some way in that "original fear" of death.

But all our strategies of self-protection are ultimately vanity, a kind of putting off of the inevitable. That awareness is the source of the existential anguish we see in the Psalter and in the wisdom literature, most prominently in the book of Ecclesiastes.

> For the fate of the sons of men and the fate of beasts is the same; as one dies, so dies the other... for all is vanity. All go to one place; all are from the dust, and all turn to dust again.[14]

With the coming of Christ, man's fate is changed. The power of sin and death are broken. Death is no longer our inevitable end. "Formerly, death awaited you as the setting sun of your life," St. Peter Chrysologus said. "He wants you to have a new birth of life."[15] So that we might have this new birth, Jesus clothed himself in the weakness of human flesh and blood. He shared our limitations and temptations, and experienced for himself what each of us fears the most — death. He did this, the letter to the Hebrews declares:

> that through death he might destroy him who has the power of death, that is, the devil, and deliver all those who through fear of death were subject to lifelong bondage.[16]

The power wielded by the devil is the power of death. The devil oppresses us through this knowledge that we are dust, that our lives are impermanent.[17] We are helpless before the power of death. And the fact that we know this is often the remote occasion for sin. In our weakness, in trying to avoid or distract ourselves from this reality, we become prisoners of our fears and slaves of sin.[18]

St. Paul was very aware of this psychological drama. Without the hope of the resurrection, he said, we end up living solely for comfort and pleasures — eating and drinking, trying to achieve whatever power, wealth, or control we can — "for tomorrow we die."[19] Our materialistic, consumeristic culture today can sometimes seem like it is organized solely to amuse and distract people from the reality that "tomorrow we die."

Consider the restless, insatiable appetites and lifestyles of many who live without faith in the promises of God. Lurking in the background, always, is this fear of death, the dread that this life may be all there is. Again, this is a theme found in the Bible's wisdom traditions:

> A heavy yoke is upon the sons of Adam,
> from the day they come forth from their mother's womb
> till the day they return to the mother of all.
> Their perplexities and fear of heart,
> their anxious thought is the day of death,
> from the man who sits on a splendid throne
> to the one who is humbled in dust and ashes...
> there is anger and envy and trouble and unrest,
> and fear of death.[20]

Jesus Christ lifts that heavy yoke from the children of Adam. He frees us from the bondage of the fear of death. This is one of the meanings of the exorcisms that Jesus performs in the Gospels. In casting out demons he destroys "the works of the devil."[21] The foremost of those works is "the power of death."[22]

Jesus himself described his work as binding a strong man, taking over his fortress, and capturing his possessions. In this symbolic expression, the devil is the strong man, the fortress is the world under the dominion of sin, and the strong man's "possessions" are the people in bondage to the power of death.[23]

The foundation of Christian fortitude is to be located here — in Christ's conquest of death and his setting free of human kind from the power of death. "Fear not!" is both a command and a promise. It is a summons to follow the Lord — confident that if we give our lives to him, he will give us a share in his resurrection.

Power Came Forth from Him

For the apostles, the cross was the ultimate sign of "the power of God."[24] For by the cross, Christ overcame death. He was "crucified in weakness but lives by the power of God," as Paul declared.[25]

We saw how the Old Testament portrayed God as the Almighty Creator of heaven and earth and the source of all power in the universe. This carries over into the New Testament. Jesus, under questioning from the High Priest, refers to God simply as "The Power."[26] But the New Testament also describes Jesus with attributes that the Old Testament reserves for God. He is called the "image of the invisible God," through whom the world and everything in it is created.[27] He is said to have dominion and power over the forces of nature — even the wind and the sea obey him.[28]

Isaiah said the Messiah would be called "God the mighty," and would possess the divine spirit of "might" or fortitude.[29] Jesus fulfills this prophecy. This is one of the core ideas in the apostolic preaching: "God *anointed* Jesus of Nazareth with the Holy Spirit and *with power* [and] he went about doing good and *healing all that were oppressed by the devil*, for God was with him."[30]

According to the apostles' preaching, Jesus is the power of God made flesh, the embodiment of God's power: "Salvation and the power ... of our God ... have come."[31] Just touching his human body communicated to those who believed the very power of God. "Power came forth from him and he healed them all," we read in the Gospel of Luke.[32]

Christ passed on this power to his apostles. The Twelve were "clothed with power from on high,"[33] and given a share in his power and authority over "all the power of the enemy."[34] Jesus gave the Twelve the strength and authority to do what he did — to preach the Word with power, to heal the sick, to cast out demons, to celebrate the Eucharist and forgive sins, even to raise the dead.

Though we see individual apostles filled with the power of God, working great miracles,[35] they were all keenly aware that their strength was not their own. "Those men who received power from God never used that power as if it were their own, but referred the power to him from whom they received it," observed St. John Cassian. "For the power itself derived its force from the same source as its origin, and it could not be given through the instrumentality of the ministers unless it had come from the Author."[36]

This is an important point. The power of the apostles was "instrumental." They knew they were instruments of the power of Christ. When Peter healed the lame man at the Temple gate, he insisted the miracle was not the result of "our own power or piety." Rather, the man was raised "by the name of Jesus Christ of Nazareth ... crucified whom God raised from the dead."[37] Paul, too, credited everything he did to "what Christ has *wrought through me* ... by the power of the Holy Spirit."[38]

Ordination and the Priesthood of the Apostles

The power given to the apostles is passed on, through the laying on of hands, to the priest. We, too are clothed with power from on high and made capable of communicating

Christ's own salvation and power through our preaching and through the sacraments.

I need to underline what I said in the last chapter: God does not bestow his power upon us for its own sake. We are ordained in his power in order to serve his covenant plan. And it is important that we understand that the priesthood, the ordained ministry, was a part of God's plan for his new covenant from the beginning. As we noted in the last chapter, the New Testament envisions the apostles as "priests of the new covenant," in continuity with the old covenant priesthood.[39]

Mark's account of the apostles' selection actually uses the language of "priestly" ordination found in the Old Testament. The meaning is clear. Jesus is passing on his own sacred power, a share in his own priesthood, which was expressed most perfectly in his sacrificial offering of himself on the cross. The Jesuit theologian of the priesthood, Father Jean Galot, has observed:

> Mark takes pains to emphasize that there is something of a creation in the initiative of Jesus. He says: "He *made* Twelve of them.... He *made* the Twelve" (Mark 3:14, 16).... The verb "to make" suggests by association the verb that appears in the Genesis account of the first creation, and again in Isaiah (Isa. 43:1; 44:2) with reference to the establishment of God's people....
>
> Note more specifically that the Semitic usage of the verb "to make" with persons as objects occurs three times in the Old Testament. In 1 Kings 13:33 and 2 Chronicles 13:9 we have the phrase "to *make* priests," and in 1 Samuel 12:6 the statement: "[the LORD] *made* Moses and Aaron." The expression "to make a priest" or "to make priests" reappears in the New Testament (Heb. 3:2; Rev. 5:10). The verb used by Mark is particularly apt to point

to the creation of the new priesthood, even if the word "priest" does not appear in the account.[40]

The powers that Christ gave to his apostles are *priestly* powers. The apostolic work that he sent them out to do was *priestly*. Essentially, they are the powers to mediate God's presence and power to the people. The apostles, as Pope Benedict XVI has said, are consecrated by Christ as "the priests of the new covenant."[41] This is very important to acknowledge. For in the years since Vatican II it has often been wrongly argued that the priesthood is a later development in the Church and that there is little evidence for a "new Testament priesthood."[42]

To the contrary, while the specific terminology may be lacking, a close reading of the New Testament indicates a well-developed sense of priestly identity among the first ministers of the Gospel. This is especially clear in the writings of St. Paul. His priestly self-understanding is vividly expressed in his letter to the Romans, where he speaks of

the grace given me by God to be a *minister* of Christ Jesus to the Gentiles in the *priestly service* of the Gospel of God, so that the *offering* of the Gentiles may be *acceptable, sanctified* by the Holy Spirit.[43]

This language deliberately suggests priestly responsibilities. The emphasized terms are all derived from Israel's sacrificial cult. The word "minister," comes from the Greek *leitourgon*, which is where we get our word "liturgy." It implies a liturgical, ritual leader. The curious expression, "priestly service," does not appear anywhere else in the New Testament and only in one place in the Greek translation of the Old. It translates the verb *hierourgein*, which means "to function as a priest," and elsewhere in Jewish literature is used to refer to the work of Israel's priests in the Temple.[44]

Pope Benedict has identified this passage from Romans as a key to understanding the essentially priestly and liturgical identity of Paul's ministry, and hence its connection to the priesthood today.

> In this verse alone does Paul use the word "*hierourgein*" — to administer as a priest — together with "*leitourgos*" — liturgy. He speaks of the cosmic liturgy in which the human world itself must become worship of God, an oblation in the Holy Spirit. When the world in all its parts has become a liturgy of God, when in its reality it has become adoration, then it will have reached its goal and will be safe and sound. This is the ultimate goal of St. Paul's apostolic mission as well as of our own mission. The Lord calls us to this ministry... to become true liturgists of Jesus Christ.[45]

Paul sees his apostolic work in priestly terms. Elsewhere, he speaks of his "ministry of reconciliation" — a role reserved in the Old Testament for priests, who brought about the forgiveness of sins through the expiating sacrifices of the Temple. Paul also described himself as an "ambassador of Christ."[46] In rabbinic thought, an ambassador literally *re-presented* his client. And Paul was received by the churches "as an angel of God, *as Christ Jesus*."[47]

This is important, too, for understanding the powers of the priesthood and their essential relationship to the power of Christ. In his sacramental ministry — for instance, in forgiving sins — Paul said he acted "in the presence of Christ (*en prosopo Christou*)."[48] The Greek term here, *prosopo*, literally means "face," but can also mean "person" or "presence." It was understood in the early Church as signifying a radical *re-presentation* of Christ, a communicating of his power. Hence, in the fourth century, when St. Jerome made his translation of the Scriptures, he translated the phrase with the Latin expression "*in persona Christi*" — "in the person of Christ."

This is how Paul understood the apostolic ministry — as manifesting the presence, the person, and the face of Jesus Christ, the new High Priest.[49] The power to do this, to serve *in persona Christi,* is the "gift of God" that is transmitted through the laying on of hands in ordination.[50]

This short excursus on the New Testament priesthood is intended to confirm that Christ still "makes priests" today by the sacrament of ordination. In the New Testament the solemn gesture of the laying on of hands is associated with the conferral of divine power.[51] And in the bishop's laying on of hands at ordination, these powers of Christ come upon the ordained. We confess this in the prayers of the ordination rite:

> Let us pray that God the *all-powerful* Father will pour out abundantly the gifts of heaven on this, his servant, whom he has chosen for the office of priest....
>
> Hear us, we beseech you, Lord our God, and pour out on this servant of yours the blessing of the Holy Spirit and *the power* of priestly grace....[52]

The powers given to the priest by ordination are a sharing in the power of God for the salvation of the world. The priest's powers, like those of the apostles, are "instrumental." Christ promised Peter, the prince of the apostles, that through the apostolic ministry the Church would prevail over "the powers of death."[53]

The priestly powers entrusted to the Church are in the service of that end — Christ's final triumph over the last enemy, death.[54] The priest, like St. Paul, is commissioned to turn people from "the power of Satan to God."[55] Like the first disciples, he is given authority over "the power of the enemy." And in our priestly ministry, Jesus sees Satan falling like lighting.[56]

But the powers given to the priest are not only those that enable him to be Christ's instrument in preaching, governing, teaching, and sanctifying. The priest is also given "interior" powers and strength. Though not identified by name, the New Testament does seem to recognize the gift of the Spirit as including an interior power very much like what later theology would call the gift of fortitude or the infused virtue of fortitude.

> The gift of God ... is *within you* through the laying on of my hands, for God did not give us a Spirit of cowardice but *a Spirit of power and love and self-control.*[57]

The Lord strengthens the hearts of those who serve him, through the "spiritual gift" of grace imparted by his Spirit.[58] This is a theme that runs throughout the apostolic writings. The gift of divine strength is given to strengthen what Paul calls "the inner man." Thus Paul can pray that we be *"strengthened* with might through his Spirit in *the inner man* ... by *the power at work within us."*[59] This gift is a participation in God's own power, and it seems especially associated with strengthening the believer to endure hardship and suffering for the sake of the Gospel.

> May you be strengthened with all power according to his glorious might, for all endurance and patience with joy.[60]

> And after you have suffered a little while, the God of all grace, who has called you ... will himself ... strengthen you.[61]

The New Testament testifies to the apostles' newfound courage after receiving the gift of the Spirit at Pentecost. In the immediate days after the arrest and torture of Jesus, they cowered behind locked doors. Following the descent of the Spirit, they are shown going forth boldly to proclaim the Gospel in the face of hostility and persecution. At Pentecost, "the Holy Spirit fills them with *fortitude,*" says the Benedictine spiritual master, Blessed Columba Marmion.[62] There is power in the apostles' words and fearlessness in their proclamation. Later, when they were brought before the Sanhedrin and beaten, the apostles "rejoic[ed] that they were counted worthy to suffer" for Jesus and his Gospel.[63]

"I can do all things in him who strengthens me," Paul declared.[64] And his litany of hardships and sufferings included imprisonments, beatings to the point of death, stonings, shipwreck, and "the daily pressure upon me of my anxiety for all the churches."[65]

So we see that great power and courage was available to the apostles. That power and courage is also available, through the laying on of hands by the successors of the apostles, to those who share in their priestly ministry down through the ages. This power includes not only the authority and ability to perform the "works" that Jesus performed for the sake of salvation,[66] but also the interior gift of fortitude, or divine strengthening of the "inner man," that makes the priestly ministry possible.

The Paradox of Power in the New Testament

Yet there is a paradox at the heart of the New Testament understanding of power. God does not manifest himself in cosmic signs and wonders. Rather, his divine power is manifested in weakness, humiliation, and destruction — in the failure of the cross. As Paul testified, in "Christ crucified" we see "the power of God."[67]

The Greeks and Romans, with their aggressively physical and martial ideas about manliness and courage, considered this preaching to be foolishness. The Jews, expecting a mighty Messiah, found it scandalous. But the cross remains the only key to understanding God's power, as well as his love. In turn, the cross is essential to understanding the source of the priest's powers — and what Pope John Paul called the essential truth about the priesthood of Christ and our own priesthood.

The cross is the sign of the mystery of a God who suffers human weakness in order to show that "the weakness of God is stronger than men."[68] The Gospel we proclaim in the Church is nothing other than "the word of the cross."[69] And Christ's whole life was a "word of the cross." His death marked the end of an earthly life that shared in all the weaknesses and limitations of our human condition, beginning with his incarnation.

Jesus came, not in power and glory, but unable to speak or walk, incapable of feeding or defending himself. His first nine months were spent in the most helpless and utterly dependent of human conditions — that of an unborn child. And throughout the Gospel, he is "beset by weakness," experiencing in his flesh all of our ordinary lacks and diminishments, except for sin.[70]

St. Thomas Aquinas said Christ came among us in "a state of weakness," so that there would be no doubt that his teaching was from God.

> For if he were rich, powerful and established in high dignity, it could be thought that his teaching and his miracles were received on account of his favor and human power. So to make the work of divine power apparent, he chose everything that was rejected and low in the world — a poor mother and a poor life, illiterate disciples and messengers, and allowed himself to be rebuked and condemned even to death by the magnates of this world. This made it apparent that his miracles and teaching were not received because of human power, but should be attributed to divine power.[71]

In humbling himself to accept death on the cross, Jesus showed us definitively that true power comes, not in willful self-assertion, but in freely aligning our will with the will of

God the Father, in an attitude of filial love and obedience.[72] Christ's humble obedience in love to the Father is the central drama of the Gospel.

Out of love, he emptied himself to come down and dwell among us.[73] He said he had come for just one purpose: to do his Father's will.[74] The lesson he leaves us is summarized in his prayer of self-offering to the Father, repeated three times during his agony in the garden: "Not as I will, but as you will."[75] This attitude of humble obedience to the Father's will is a distinctive mark of Christ's human personality. As the great German theologian of the twentieth century, Father Romano Guardini, wrote:

> Jesus' entire existence is *the translation of power into humility* ... [and] into obedience to the will of the Father. Obedience is not secondary for Jesus, but forms the core of his being.[76]

To receive his power and strength, the priest must accept it in humility, giving himself in love to the Father as Jesus did. "Imitate Jesus Christ as he imitated the Father," said the holy priest and bishop, St. Ignatius of Antioch.[77] The imitation of Christ, *imitatio Christi,* is at the core of apostolic spirituality presented in the New Testament. This is a consistent theme in the writings of St. Paul: "Be imitators of me, as I am of Christ."[78]

In washing the apostles' feet at the Last Supper, Jesus said: "I have given you an example, that you also should do as I have done."[79] The example that Christ gave to his apostles and to his priests is *the translation of power into humility.* And this spirituality, this *imitatio Christi,* must shape the character of our apostolic ministry as priests. The priesthood has very little to do with power, as the world understands power. It has everything to do with sacrifice. Christ compared it to the work of a shepherd. "The good shepherd lays down his life for the sheep" — as a good father loves and protects his family; as a husband loves and provides for his wife. God asks every priest to do the same. When Jesus said, "I am the good shepherd," he gave us the words that should shape our lives as priests.[80]

In marriage, a man and woman change — not only in what they do and how they live, but in who they are. The sacrament makes them one flesh. The covenant binds them into one life lived for each other, for their children, and for the world. And so it is for the priest. Ordination changes who we are. It shapes us — *in persona Christi* — in the person of Christ, so that his life and his love become *our* life and *our* love.

Our service is never a job and never a profession. Those are words that describe a hireling, a shepherd who works for pay. What we are called to in our vocation is much more radical than that. A good father loves without counting the cost. A good husband loves as Jesus loved us from the cross. And a good priest does the same. He leads his people in the truth of Jesus Christ, faithful to the teachings of Christ's Church and obedient to the needs of the people Jesus died to save.

Power Made Perfect in Weakness

A priest once asked the Catholic novelist and Nobel laureate, François Mauriac, to write something about the priesthood. Mauriac replied:

> What does the priest mean to me? The meeting of the power of God and the weakness of a mortal being in one and the same person.[81]

This is a good definition of the priesthood in its essential mystery. By ordination we "take on the likeness of Christ,"[82] who in himself joined the power of the God to the weakness of human flesh. To again quote the beautiful reflections of St. Thomas:

> In what he did or suffered, human weakness and divine power were joined together at the same time. Thus at his nativity he was wrapped in cloth and put in a manger, but praised by the angels and adored by the Magi led by a star. He was tempted by the devil, but ministered to by angels. He lived without money as a beggar, but raised the dead and gave sight to the blind. He died fixed to the cross and numbered among thieves, but at his death the sun darkened, the earth trembled, stones split, graves opened and the bodies of the dead were raised.[83]

We who are privileged to be instruments of his divine power, in our imitation of Christ will find his strength in our weakness. The gift of divine strength, fortitude, is given to us for the love of God. Augustine called the priesthood the *amoris officium,* the office of love.[84] And the holy patron of priests, the Curé d'Ars, St. John Vianney, said: "The priesthood is the love of the heart of Jesus."[85]

God gives courage to priests that we might love more completely. St. Theodoret of Cyr said: "Grace was given to us so *that we might not be afraid but love all the more* steadily."[86] This is the reason for fortitude in the life of the priest. As we have said, the "new commandment" of love called for by Jesus *presumes the gift of fortitude* that enables us to face death without fear. How else could he command this kind of love: "This is my commandment, that you love one another as I have loved you. Greater love has no man than this, that a man lay down his life for his friends."[87]

In fact, the only New Testament use of the verb form for "fortitude" is found in an exhortation to complete love. "Be courageous. Be strong. Let all you do be done in love," Paul exhorts the Corinthians.[88] Even martyrdom, Paul said, if not entered into in love, is not worthy of the name.[89]

The Content and Certitude of Christian Hope

This brings us to contemplate what is ultimately distinctive about Christian fortitude. And that is the virtue of hope. Christian hope is not a species of wishful thinking or an optimistic outlook about the future. Our hope has a specific content and certitude. It is hope in the resurrection, established by the sure knowledge of Christ's own resurrection and the promise of our own. The priest, with Paul, possesses "hope of eternal life which God, who never lies, promised ages ago."[90]

The content and certitude of this hope is what makes Christian fortitude unique. Whatever beliefs the Greeks and Romans had about the afterlife, there is nothing in those traditions that resembles Christian certainty and hope in the resurrection. In any event, Hellenistic beliefs about the afterlife are not a factor in their thinking about the virtues. The case is a bit more complicated in Jewish thought. We saw in the moving tale of the seven Maccabees, and we see again in the New Testament, evidence of Jewish belief in the resurrection.[91] However, until Christ, no one had come back from the dead.[92]

The resurrection is decisive for Christian fortitude. If fortitude is fearlessness in the face of death and readiness to die in battle, Christian fortitude is fearlessness and readiness founded on the sure knowledge that Christ has risen and that we, too, will rise. Christ is the "firstfruits" of all who will rise from the dead.[93] He is the "pioneer and perfecter of our faith."[94]

Because of this we, too, can be bold in our ministry, knowing that joy awaits those who endure suffering and shame for the sake of the Gospel. Hope in the resurrection is the basis for the apostles' bravery and daring. As Paul said:

For he was crucified in weakness, but lives by the power of God. For we are weak in him, but... we shall live with him by the power of God.[95]

By faith in the resurrection, the priest can endure the cross of his ministry. With the same power given to the apostles, the priest can endure insults, hardships, persecutions, and calamities — all for the sake of Christ. In this, he experiences an ever deeper identification with our Lord. The power of Christ is made even more manifest in his person, as he understands what Jesus told Paul in his sufferings: "My grace is sufficient for you, for *my power is made perfect in weakness.*" The priest understands that in living by grace alone, in the weakness of his flesh, he becomes a vessel for Christ's power to manifest itself. He can say with Paul, "I will not boast, except of my weakness.... For when I am weak, then I am strong."[96]

In the final book of the Bible, in his revelation to St. John, Jesus says: "Be not afraid!... I died, and behold I am alive for evermore, and I have the keys to death."[97] From start to finish, the New Testament is a catechesis in fortitude, a catechesis in courage. As Pope John Paul said in his talk on the virtue:

The Gospel is addressed to weak, poor, meek and humble men, peacemakers and to the merciful, but, at the same time, it contains a constant appeal to fortitude. It often repeats: "Fear not" (Matt. 14:27). It teaches man that — for a just cause, for truth, for justice — one must be able to "lay down one's life" (John 15:13).[98]

The promise of the resurrection is a call to fearless proclamation and witness to the Gospel. The hope of the resurrection should wipe away all our fears of death. "Be not afraid, only believe!" Jesus declares throughout the Gospels. The promise of the Lord is that he who endures until the end will be saved.

His apostles, especially, and those who carry on the apostolic ministry, are assured:

> In the world you have tribulation; but be of good cheer. I have overcome the world.[99]

CHAPTER 6

The Image of God and the Perfection of Virtue

Aspects of St. Thomas Aquinas's Christian Humanism

Sᴛ. Tʜᴏᴍᴀs Aǫᴜɪɴᴀs ᴡᴀs a man of such towering intellectual accomplishments that we can easily forget that he was also a humble and holy priest, whose preaching often moved people to tears.

His earliest biographers paint a portrait of a man of great personal character and virtue. One story that is always told is about how his mother, the Dame Theodora of Theate, opposed the 19-year-old Thomas's decision to join the Dominicans. She had him kidnapped and held him against his will for more than a year in one of the family's fortresses. During this time, various family members begged Thomas to change his mind — all to no avail.

As a last resort, the family retained a beautiful prostitute and sent her to Thomas's chambers to entice him to sin. The plan failed miserably. Thomas chased her from his room, waving a hot iron he had pulled from the fireplace. He then used the iron to burn the sign of the cross on the wooden door.

This story is usually retold as an example of Thomas's commitment to the virtue of chastity. It is most certainly that. But it is also a testimony to Thomas's fortitude, his strength of character, and his fearless endurance in following the call of the Lord. His entire time locked away in that fortress was a

125

testament to his ability to resist temptation and endure hardship and humiliation in the service of Jesus Christ.

Thomas was a man of great virtue. We cannot forget this as we begin our study of his profound teaching on the virtues. Because Thomas lived what he taught. Or better: Thomas taught what he lived. There was no conflict between his study of sacred Scripture and doctrine and his life of prayer and ascetic discipline.

Joseph Pieper has wisely observed the connection between Thomas's spiritual life and his intellectual quest for the truth.

> [W]e have lost the awareness of the close bond that links the knowing of truth to the condition of purity. Thomas says that unchastity's firstborn daughter is blindness of the spirit. Only he who wants nothing for himself, who is not subjectively "interested," can know the truth. On the other hand, an impure, selfishly corrupted will-to-pleasure destroys both resoluteness of spirit and the ability of the psyche to listen in silent attention to the language of reality.[1]

Thomas understood himself as a servant of the truth that God had revealed to him in his own life. He wrote: "For my own part, I envisage, as the main duty of my life, the working out of my debt to God in such a way that I express him in my every word and attitude."[2] The Dominican theologian, Cardinal Yves Congar, said this mission to express the truth defined the "spiritual essence" of the man. "His whole life was to be an utterance of God."[3]

G. K. Chesterton, in his classic biography, *The Dumb Ox*, observed that Thomas, "more than he is anything else, is a great anthropologist." What Chesterton meant is that Thomas's theological and philosophical project was based on his understanding of the mystery of the human person in God's plan for creation. Thomas's intellectual and spiritual inquiry into this mystery resulted in what Chesterton rightly described as "a complete theory of man."[4]

This is a crucial insight. And that is why, before discussing Thomas's teaching on fortitude and the priesthood, I think it is necessary in this chapter to try to sketch the broader outlines of Thomas's anthropology. This broader theory of man, as well as Thomas's teaching on the specific virtue of courage, reflects the fruitful encounter of Greek philosophy and the Gospel. And I believe this teaching has much to contribute to the spiritual and moral development of priests and men training for the priesthood today.

Again, I should emphasize that my purposes in this book are pastoral, not strictly theological or philosophical. My intention is not to present a scholarly treatise on Thomas. Rather, I hope to recover some of the basics of his teaching as a guide for priestly formation and spiritual growth. As others have pointed out, Thomas's great synthesis of faith and reason is deeply "evangelical," pressing the insights of Greek and Roman moral philosophy into service of the Gospel's goals of leading people beyond mere philosophical wisdom and toward "Christlikeness."[5]

Living as the *Imago Dei*

Thomas articulates a rich and complex theory of the human person — embracing mind and heart, body and soul, thought and action, emotion and passion, faith and reason, sensory perception and moral decision-making. I cannot hope to do justice to this theory in these next few pages. But I would like to identify certain aspects of his anthropology that will be fruitful for understanding his treatment of the virtues, especially the virtue of fortitude.

His anthropology begins and ends with our creation *imago Dei*. For Thomas, the biblical fact of our creation in "the image and likeness of God"[6] is "the basis for our participation in the divine life."[7] That means that, as God is an intelligent being with the capacity for free action, capable also of knowing and loving himself, we too possess intelligence, freedom, and a natural aptitude to know and love God.[8]

For Thomas, the *imago* is not a static thing, a "given" quality we possess by virtue of being human. The *imago* orients our lives toward the goal and purpose of our creation. To be created in the image of God is to be made for God — for beatitude, for the blessedness of God's own life.

Thomas seemed to envision a dynamic transformation of the image of God in us — from the image of God given to us by our nature (*natura*), to the image of God made possible by the grace given to us in Christ (*gratia*), to the final image of God to be realized by our participation in the Trinitarian life in the glory of heaven (*gloria*).[9]

The image of nature, the image in which we are created, gives us the capacity to know and love God. This remains in everyone, even though the image of God in us has been distorted by original sin and by our own sins. Jesus Christ, the Son and true image of God[10] come down in human likeness,[11] restores what was damaged by sin, through his obedient suffering and death on the cross. By the grace and new life of divine sonship in the Spirit granted to us in the resurrected Christ, humanity is once again able to realize and perfect the image of God in which we were created.[12]

Thomas gives us an overarching vision of the continual perfection, under grace and the Spirit, of the image of God in the human person. His vision is finely reflected in these words from the *Catechism:* "The vocation of humanity is to show forth the image of God and to be transformed into the image of the Father's only Son."[13] As Thomas himself said: "The ultimate end of things is to become like God."[14]

A Creature of Powers and Appetites

Created in the image of God and destined for blessed communion with God, the human person for Thomas is a unity of body and soul, with the soul giving form to the body. Thomas's teaching on the capacities and makeup of the human person or soul is always set in the context of our creation in God's image. The *imago* means that the human person is an intelligent being endowed with free will and the power to control his actions.[15] Among the creations of God, the human person alone can have dominion over his acts, dominion that he achieves through the operations of his intelligence and will.

Thomas states that "everything that acts, acts in order to [achieve] its purposes."[16] That is because God is the first cause of all things in creation, imprinting upon every agent an ordination to its purpose. "Hence all things that exist, in whatsoever manner, are necessarily directed by God towards some end."[17]

Man's happiness — his purpose or "last end" — is the possession of God. The goal of the moral life is what Thomas calls friendship with God.

> Charity signifies not only the love of God, but also a certain friendship with him; which implies, besides love, a certain mutual return of love, together with mutual communion.... Now this fellowship with God, which consists in a certain colloquy with him, is begun here, in this life, by grace, but will be perfected in the future life, by glory.[18]

To ensure that we achieve that end, God created us with various "powers" of the soul that must be ordered to their appropriate end, namely, to the attainment of our happiness in God.[19] In Thomas's view, we attain God and our happiness in this life through the free and rational choices of our intelligence and will, guided by a will oriented to God.[20] As the Dominican theologian Father M. D. Chenu has explained, for Thomas, human acts are "so many steps by which human nature on its journey back to the source of its being realizes its end, thereby achieving happiness and perfection."[21]

Of course, it is not by our works alone that we attain God. As Thomas insists, "by God alone is man made happy, if we speak of perfect happiness."[22] Yet if ultimately God "makes" us happy — through the truths he has revealed and the grace he bestows upon us in Christ — there is a great field of human action in which we are called to respond to his grace and truth. This field of action is the precise domain of the virtues, including courage.

But before we consider the virtues, we need to account for the other "powers" Thomas identifies in the makeup of the human soul. He recognizes certain lower powers that humans share with all living things. These are the *vegetative* powers that enable the person to generate, nurture, grow, and conserve his life.[23]

We also possess *sensitive* or *sensory* powers or faculties, including the five exterior senses of sight, hearing, touch, taste, and smell. In addition, we have certain interior sensory powers — common sense, imagination, estimation, and memory — by which we organize and make judgments about what we apprehend by the senses.

Notable here is the *sensus communis,* or common sense, by which we are able to gather and distinguish the information we receive from our senses. Also notable is the "estimative power" (*via aestimativa*), which enables us to make judgments about whether the things we perceive are useful or friendly on the one hand, or potentially harmful on the other.[24]

In addition to the vegetative and sensitive powers, the human person also possesses faculties of the *intellect*[25] and *appetite,*[26] each of which is intended by God to orient the person to the love of the truth and the love of what is good. The intellect is our power to know things and to acquire knowledge of things. This power of the soul relies on a number of different distinctly human capacities that enable us to retain knowledge and to organize and compare the things we know in order to form new judgments and objects of knowledge. In God's plan for the human person, the intellect is meant to be ordered to seek the truth about God's creation.

In our pursuit of knowledge concerning the ultimate truth, God, we are aided by the additional gift of *faith.* Faith, according to Thomas, is an act of the intellect that enables us to know far more than what we could apprehend by the operations of our senses and reason alone.[27] Moreover, faith is necessary to know those things revealed by God that are necessary to our true happiness.[28]

Thomas also considers the *conscience* to be a part of our intellectual capacities.[29] Conscience, essentially, is "the application of knowledge or science to what we do," he says. In other words, conscience involves acts of judgment — as to what is right or wrong, or what we should or should not do — that are based on knowledge we already possess, including the natural law that God has written into our hearts.[30]

In addition to our intellectual powers, we are creatures of *appetite.* The "appetitive power of the soul" is what enables man to desire the things he apprehends by his senses and his intellect. There is a *natural* appetite — for food, drink, and the other necessities of physical life. There is also *sensuality* or the *sensitive* appetite — "the appetite of things belonging to the body."[31]

Aquinas divides this latter appetite into two powers — the *concupiscible* and the *irascible.* The concupiscible desires what is good for us and avoids what is not. The irascible both defends us against what threatens our attainment of the good and helps us to overcome obstacles to the good. These powers of the soul are intended by God to be guided and directed by our reason.

We also possess a *rational appetite* or *will*.[32] Decisive here is our *free will*, which according to Thomas, is a chief aspect of the image of God in us, and the power of our appetite that enables us to make free choices with regards to both our intentions and our actions. By the gift of free will, we make judgments based on our perceptions of the world, freely deciding to seek the good or to avoid the bad. Indeed, there is true freedom only when we, through free intentional decisions and actions, order our entire being to the purpose for which we are created. However, because of original sin, we can abuse this divine gift and use our freedom to pursue disordered purposes or to give free reign to our disordered passions.

God does not leave us alone in our freedom. Indeed, Thomas says that "free will is not sufficient.... unless it be moved and helped by God."[33] We are free to put ourselves under the subject of grace, by which God helps us to choose what is good.[34] For Thomas, "grace is nothing other than the beginning of glory in us."[35]

The Passions and the Virtues

According to Thomas's complex and sophisticated understanding of the human person, we are also creatures of passion and emotion. In his typical analytical fashion, Thomas identifies eleven basic passions related to the sensory appetites of the soul — distinguishing these passions by whether they correspond to our *concupiscible* or *irascible* appetites.

The concupiscible appetites include love, hate, desire, aversion, joy, and sorrow. They are best understood as "passions of attraction" or "impulse emotions,"[36] because they relate to our instinctive tendency to seek what is pleasurable to the body and the senses and to avoid what might be painful.[37] On the other hand, our irascible appetites are "passions of attack" or "contentious emotions"[38] — namely, hope, despair, fear, courage, and anger. These passions are responses aroused by our confrontation with what we perceive to be evil, difficult, or threatening to our well-being.

Our passions and emotions, as with everything about us, are intended in God's plan to be subordinated — to be put under the direction of our reason and ordered to our attainment of happiness, which, as we have said, rests ultimately in friendship with God. Because of the wounds of original sin, however, the control of our passions requires constant ascetical discipline and training. This was recognized by St. Paul's famous admission: "I do not understand my own actions.... I can will what is right, but I cannot do it."[39]

In his Christian anthropology, Thomas, too, has an acute perception of this struggle. He makes his own a vivid metaphor from Aristotle to say that we control our emotions and appetites much as a political ruler governs free and sometimes unruly subjects:

> The body is ruled by the soul, and the irascible and concupiscible powers by reason, but in different ways.... Aristotle says that reason rules the irascible and concupiscible powers with political control, as free men are ruled who have in some matters a will of their own. This is why *virtues* are required in these powers, so that they may be well fitted for operation.[40]

Here we enter into the centrality of the *virtues* in Thomas's understanding of the Christian life. We have seen that for Thomas we are complex creatures composed of body and soul, with various powers, appetites, passions, and emotions, who express ourselves through acts of intellect and will. We have further seen that for Thomas we are made in the image of God — created with a kind of in-born vocation to perfect that *imago Dei* by conforming ourselves to the *imago Christi,* who manifested in human flesh the perfect image of the invisible God.

The key question of our existence then becomes: how are we to conform ourselves to the image of Christ, and thereby to perfect the image of God in us and to obtain the participation in the divine blessedness for which we are made? The solution must be to find some way to order our passions, thoughts, and actions to lead us to happiness in this life and eternal life with God.

For, as Thomas continually stresses, our happiness is not found in worldly things such as pleasures, honors, power, or wealth. "It is impossible for any created good to constitute man's happiness," he says. "This is to be found not in any creature, but in God alone."[41]

This is where the *virtues,* especially the moral virtues, come into play. The virtues, for Thomas, are good habits or dispositions by which we are made capable of perfecting the image of God in us by becoming more like Christ. And in this we achieve our happiness and, ultimately, the vision of God. "Man is perfected by virtue, for those actions whereby he is directed to happiness," says Thomas.[42] Again, he stresses: "The spiritual life is perfected by the virtues, since it is by them that we lead a good life."[43]

Virtus and *Habitus*

Thomas, following the Latin meaning of *virtus,* defines virtue essentially as habit that brings about the perfection of some power or faculty of the soul.[44] The life of virtue, as it was for the ancients, was the noblest form of living for Thomas.

The centerpiece of Thomas's "realist anthropology" is the notion of *habitus.* It is important to know that for Thomas, *habitus* means more than our commonplace idea of "habit" as a pattern of expected behavior created by repeated actions. "Habits are perfections," qualities that dispose a person to realize the necessary purposes of his faculties.[45] The habits of the virtues operate in such a way that our ordinary faculties or powers are inclined to the truth, to the good, and to God.

As Dominican Father Romanus Cessario has written, *habitus* "supposes a conception of the human person as open to development and modification from both natural and divine causes."[46] *Habitus* is a principle of growth. It means that through our activity, our free choice, the use of our intelligence, we can master our actions and grow in virtue. This becomes an important premise in our final chapter when we consider formation and education in the virtue.

We are not born with virtues, but they can be learned or, in Thomas's formulation, *acquired*. Among the acquired human virtues, he distinguishes *intellectual virtues*, that aim at perfecting the use of our reason, and *moral virtues*, that aim at the perfection of our appetites, especially the will. In his *Summa Theologiae*, Thomas discusses 53 distinct virtues, grouped around the three theological virtues of the Christian tradition — faith, hope, and charity — and the four "cardinal" virtues of the classical philosophical tradition: prudence, justice, temperance, and courage.[47]

Thus, Thomas agrees with the classical tradition that we have considered in earlier chapters — namely, that there are four "cardinal" virtues upon which the moral life of the human person hinges. In his treatment, *prudence* aims to perfect human reason so that we choose what is good for us and determine the proper means to achieving it. *Justice* aims to perfect our will so that we seek what is genuinely good for our neighbor and render to God all that we owe to him. *Temperance* aims to perfect the concupiscible appetite by curbing our desires and attractions to the good things of this world that are pleasurable to our senses. *Fortitude* aims to perfect the irascible appetite, emboldening us and strengthening us to pursue truth and goodness in the face of obstacles and dangers.

Thomas provides a very practical vision of how the cardinal virtues function in our moral life:

> As Aristotle says, "a virtue is what makes the one who has it good, and good too his activity." But the good of man is to be in accord with reason.... It follows that human virtues make a human being and his activity to be in accord with reason. This happens in three ways. First, reason itself is rectified or made right. This is done through the intellectual virtues [chiefly, through *prudence*]. Secondly, human affairs are to be put into the order required by reason. This rectitude is instituted by the virtue of *justice*. In a third way, human activity is to be made to accord with reason through the removal of obstacles or impediments.
>
> Now, the human will is hindered in two ways from following right reason. First, through being so strongly attracted to some object of pleasure that it fails to bring about the good required by reason. This impediment is removed by the virtue of *temperance*. The will is also kept from doing what reason requires on account of some difficulty that it encounters. In order to remove this obstacle, the virtue of *fortitude*, or courage of the mind, is required. By this virtue, the person resists this difficulty, just as through bodily courage, the man overcomes impediments in his physical environment.[48]

Thomas believes the human virtues have their original "types" or *exemplar* in the being of God. This is a critical and often overlooked point. Thomas builds his discussion on a beautiful quote from St. Augustine: "The soul must follow something so that virtue can be born in it; and this something is God, and if we follow him we shall live a moral life."[49]

God is the source of the human virtues as he is the source of the image of God in man. As such, we find in God the template, the model for our own contemplation and practice of the virtues.

> [V]irtue can be considered as existing in its highest ex-emplification in God, and in this fashion we can speak of *exemplar* virtues. Thus the divine mind in God can be called *prudence*, while *temperance* is the turning of the divine attention to himself, just as in us temperance is that which conforms the concupisciple appetite to reason. The *fortitude* of God is his immutability, while God's justice is the observance of the eternal law in his works.[50]

Partakers of the Divine Nature by Infused Virtue

The cardinal virtues are rooted in and inspired by the great *theological virtues* of faith, hope, and love. The theological virtues are given to us that we might achieve the happiness that surpasses our human nature — happiness which, according to Thomas, "man can obtain by the power of God alone, by a kind of participation of the Godhead, about which it is written (2 Pet. 1:4) that by Christ we are made *partakers of the divine nature.*"[51]

The theological virtues are given to perfect our relationship with God, elevating and transforming us, enabling us to live out the promise of divine sonship that comes to us in Jesus Christ. One might say that faith, hope, and love are the characteristics of the child of God.

Faith enables us to believe in the truth of God and all that he has revealed to us about himself and creation, especially through the incarnation of his only Son. *Hope* enables us to trust in Christ's promises, especially his promise of eternal life. And *love*, or *charity*, enables us to fulfill Christ's two-fold command that we live for the love of God and the love of our neighbor as ourselves.

God bestows these theological virtues upon us in baptism, giving us our vocation to divine sonship and participation in the very life of God. To use the language of Thomas, the theological virtues are "infused" by God into our souls in order to make us capable of living as God's children and thereby directing ourselves to our supernatural end.[52]

Yet if we are to live according to these principles of divine life given to us in baptism, we must also have other habits or virtues that enable us to express these principles in our daily lives. These other virtues are likewise "infused" in us, according to Thomas. The infused moral virtues of prudence, justice, fortitude, and temperance are added to the acquired virtues to orient those virtues to their supernatural end, an end that far surpasses our ordinary human powers.[53]

Thomas's teaching about the infused virtues, which is accepted and taken up in the official teaching of Church,[54] is as powerful as it is complicated. For our purposes, I only want to highlight certain aspects of this teaching that will help us to understand the possibilities and pathways for our growth in the virtues.

Thomas maintains that these virtues are "infused" in the sense that they are placed in us in baptism by the gracious gift of the Father's mercy and love. They are infused in us for the precise purpose of empowering us and enabling us to grow and develop these virtues and thereby come to holiness and blessedness with God. This does not mean that there are no purely human virtues that can be acquired by ordinary human effort. Nor does it mean that we are only "passive" recipients of the virtues infused in us by God.

The infused virtues are an expression of God's grace, and we are meant to correspond to that grace. Indeed, Thomas certainly envisions that we are to study and practice the natural or acquired virtues of prudence, justice, temperance, and fortitude so that these virtuous habits grow in us, leading us to ever greater self-mastery and a joyful life of virtue in our human and worldly affairs.

So why is there any distinction between *acquired* human virtues and *infused* moral virtues in God's plan for the human person? Thomas in one place puts it this way:

> The infused virtues ... perfect a person for a different kind of life. In brief, the acquired virtues ready one for civil life, but the infused for a spiritual life, which comes only from grace as a result of the virtuous one's membership in the Church.[55]

Thomas wants us to remember that the "good" we are to seek is always twofold. We are called not only to lead a good, natural life according to the standards of civil society and human decency. If we were called only to that end, the cardinal virtues, as perceived and taught by the great philosophers such as Aristotle, would be sufficient. But we are called to much more.

We are called to beatitude, to the life of divine filiation ("spiritual life"). Hence, we need virtues that enable us to aspire to our higher calling. Our human abilities and faculties alone could never direct us to that perfection. Only God, through the workings of grace in the Holy Spirit, can bring this about. So the infused virtues are gifts that God gives us so that we can live as his children.

The infused virtues perfect the operations of our intellect and will, ordering them in a transcendent direction toward "the end of eternal life."[56] Moreover, according to Thomas, the more we correspond to the moral virtues infused in us by grace, the more we make them a habit in our lives, the more they can grow and increase in us — with that increase granted to us also by the gift of God's grace. Thus the infused virtues are "added to the acquired virtues to fit them for a supernatural end surpassing human powers," as the Dominican moral theologian, Father Servais Pinckaers, has written.[57]

The doctrine of infused virtue should be of great consolation in our struggles to lead a virtuous and holy life. By the infused moral virtues, our efforts are elevated by divine grace. That means that through prayer, through our constant strivings in pursuit of the virtues, and through our participation in the sacraments, we have recourse to the very help of God himself — his grace, light, and strength.[58]

Moreover, we see that the life of virtue is not about a bland following of rules and regulations. On the contrary. It is an adventure in discipleship, a participation in Christ's own life as befits a child of God. Our new life of grace, bestowed upon us by the theological virtues of faith, hope, and charity, gives our life the radical new shape and character of divine filiation. The infused virtues perfect and complete our natural strivings to lead a virtuous life. They orient everything we do to the service of God's glory and our possession of eternal beatitude.

Thomas describes the difference between the acquired and infused form of the virtues in terms of the difference between our birth as flesh and blood men and women and our rebirth in the Spirit as sons and daughters of God.

> The virtues acquired by human acts ... are dispositions whereby a man is fittingly disposed with reference to the nature whereby he is a man. The infused virtues dispose man in a higher manner and towards a higher end, and consequently in relation to some higher nature — that is, in relation to a participation of the divine nature, according to 2 Peter 1:4: "He hath given us most great and most precious promises: that by these you may be made partakers of the divine nature." And it is in respect of

receiving this nature that we are said to be born again sons of God.... As the acquired virtues enable a man to walk in accordance with the natural light of reason, so do the infused virtues enable a man to walk as befits the life of grace.[59]

By the infused virtues, God fulfills his precious promise to make us sons in his Son. The virtues we live are the virtues that Christ made manifest in his human person. Our life of virtue becomes "a real participation in the *imitatio Christi*," by which we are empowered to live as he did — our intellect, will, and appetite given in complete disposition toward the Father.[60] As Father Cessario has put it:

> The infused moral virtues assume that God has acted in human history in such a way as to make beatific fellowship with himself possible for every member of the race. This elevation of human nature's destiny requires a proportionate elevation of human nature's capacities.[61]

Again, as Thomas would remind us, the infused virtues flow from Christ, who incarnates the perfection of virtue: "Since grace was at its very best in Christ, it gave rise to virtues which perfected each of the faculties of the soul and all its activities."[62]

Here I want to return to the point made above, a point that we must return to again later when we consider the ascetical life of the priest. We are born again by grace as children of God. By consequence, we participate in God's own nature through our re-creation or regeneration in the divine image. We further participate in God's knowledge through the virtue of faith, as we participate in his love through the virtue of charity.[63] And as God is the source and *exemplar* of our human virtues, Thomas teaches that God works in us to perfect us as we strive to imitate his divine virtues.

It belongs to man to strive as much as possible to attain what is divine, as ... Scripture commends to us in many places — for example, "Be ye perfect as your heavenly Father is perfect" (Matt. 5:48). Hence we must have some virtues midway between the human virtues and the exemplar virtues, which are divine.

[Of] these intermediate virtues ... some are of those who are on their way and tending toward a likeness of what is divine, and these are called purifying or perfecting virtues. Thus *prudence*, by contemplating the things of God, counts all worldly things as nothing and directs all thoughts of the soul only to God; *temperance* puts aside the customary needs of the body so far as nature permits; *fortitude* prevents the soul from being afraid of withdrawing from bodily needs and rising to heavenly things; and *justice* brings the whole soul's accord to such a way of life.

In addition, there are the virtues of those already attaining a divine likeness, which are called *perfect* virtues. Thus *prudence* now sees nothing else but the things of God, *temperance* knows no earthly desires, *fortitude* is oblivious to the passions, and *justice*, by imitating the divine mind, is united to it by an everlasting covenant. These are the virtues we attribute to the blessed or to those in this life who are at the summit of perfection.[64]

Here we see reflected the full dynamism of Thomas's teaching on the virtues, how he envisions our lives as a progression in holiness and love of Christ in perfection of the *imago Dei*. We are called to strive for the holiness and perfection of God. The cardinal virtues, which originate as *exemplars* in God and are infused in us by grace, become the pillars of our life in Christ, and the guideposts as we seek to walk in the way of Christ toward the perfection of the divine image in us.

To put it another way: the virtues are ordered to produce in us habits and actions, made possible with the help of grace and God's Law, that conform us to the image of God as that image was revealed to us in the image of his Son.[65]

The virtues, then, help to draw us toward the purpose of our creation, the glory of our final beatitude in heaven. And in this journey, Christ, by the power of his example and the grace communicated to us in the sacraments, continues this work of transformation in us.

In our striving for virtue we are assisted, finally, by the seven Gifts of the Holy Spirit, which are given to perfect the virtues in us. The gifts represent the love of God by which we are finally borne into the very heart of the Trinitarian life. "We need the Gifts of the Spirit because our virtues, no matter how good, always fall short of the goodness of God," according to ethicist Paul Waddell.[66]

Aquinas describes the gifts as given *in adjutorium virtutuum,* "to assist the virtues."[67] They are, in the words of Father Cessario, "special divine interventions ... specific kinds of divine mediations designed to aid" the virtues.[68] The gifts of *understanding* and *knowledge* are given to perfect the virtue of faith; the gift of the *fear of the Lord* perfects hope, as *wisdom* perfects charity. The virtue of prudence is perfected by the gift of *counsel,* as *piety* is given to perfect justice, and courage is perfected by *fortitude,* and temperance by the *fear of the Lord.*[69] These gifts strengthen us and make us better able to hear and respond graciously to the promptings of God.

This is the exhilarating Thomistic vision of man, a vision that in all its essential aspects expresses the authentically Catholic vision of the human person. It is a life of grace and a life of virtue, lived in friendship with Christ and with the promise of the eternal vision of God's glory and blessedness. It is a life that was well reflected in Thomas's own priesthood.

Near the end of Thomas's life, a friend quietly observed him praying in a small chapel, on his knees before a crucifix. To his amazement, the Christ on the cross began speaking to Thomas: "You have written well of me, Thomas. What reward would you receive from me for your labors?" Thomas responded with no hesitation. "Lord, nothing but yourself."

This is the reward of the life of virtue — union with Christ, God all in all, nothing but the Lord himself.

Power Made Perfect in Weakness

*The Priesthood of Christ and the Virtue
of Fortitude in Aquinas*

IN THE LATE SECOND CENTURY, Tertullian laid down what amounts to a law of spiritual growth for the Church. "We conquer in dying," he wrote in a tract addressed to Roman governors then persecuting the Church.[1] "The more we are mown down by you, the more in number we grow. The blood of Christians is seed."[2]

The Church has always grown from the blood of Christians, shed for the love of Christ and the truth of the Gospel. In the visions of St. John in the book of Revelation, he twice sees the souls of those slain for their witness (Greek: *martyrian*) to Jesus and the Word of God. And he sees Jesus, too, like the martyrs, dressed in a white robe dipped in blood.[3]

What this means is that between Christ and his martyrs there is a special bond of blood, poured out in the love of God and in testimony to his Word. According to an early Christian document on the martyrdoms under Emperor Marcus Aurelius, some who died for the faith were reluctant to describe themselves as martyrs. "For they gladly conceded the title of martyr to Christ, the faithful and true Martyr-witness and Firstborn of the dead and Prince of the life of God."[4]

The servants have never been above their Master, and true to their Master's word, believers have always suffered hatred, misunderstanding, and violence for their beliefs. From the lives of the martyrs, sown like grains of wheat, much fruit has been borne for the Church in every age and in every part of the world.[5] This is surely true in the first evangelization of the Americas.

In our lands, as it has been always and everywhere, the first martyrs were priests. "A last tribute to the priesthood is given by the enemies of the Church," Pope Pius XI once wrote. The Church's enemies know that priests are the spiritual ties that bind the Church in unity to Christ, the Pope explained. That is why they always try to kill the priests first. "It is the priesthood they desire to be rid of; that they may clear the way for the destruction of the Church."[6]

That seemed to be the logic of the band of native Americans who killed Father Juan de Padilla in 1542, near what is now Herington, Kansas. Father de Padilla, a Franciscan missionary from Spain, traveled with the conquistadors Cortez and Coronado, but with a different purpose — to bring the souls of the native peoples to Christ. None of Father de Padilla's own words survive, but the chronicler of Coronado's expeditions describes a passionate Lenten sermon in which he "declared his zeal for the conversion of these peoples and his desire to draw them to the faith."[7]

In the region of Kansas and Nebraska, he made many converts among the Quivira Indians. But when he and his companions went to a nearby village to evangelize a rival tribe, the Quivira ambushed and attacked them. Father de Padilla is said to have faced his executioners on his knees in prayer. And it is fitting that the spot where he was killed is "almost the geographical center" of what is now the United States.[8]

Father de Padilla is believed to be the first martyr to fall on American soil. And there have been many more since then. Growing up in Mexico in the generation after the great persecution of the Church, I was inspired by the stories of those priest-martyrs who helped keep the faith alive in a very dark time. One of the most inspiring stories for me was that of Blessed Miguel Pro. The courageous Jesuit priest was executed before a Mexican firing squad in 1927. As they killed him, he had his arms spread wide, and he was shouting his final witness to the faith: *"¡Viva Cristo Rey!"* ("Long live Christ the King!").

When the Church was outlawed in Mexico in the 1920s, and believers faced torture and death for the practice of the faith, Father Miguel became an underground priest, using clever disguises and staying in a series of secret "safehouses." Dressed sometimes like a mechanic and other times like a dashing playboy, he rode about Mexico City on his brother's bike. He would hear confessions, celebrate Mass in secret, distribute alms to the poor, and encourage the faithful to persevere. All the time, he was hunted by authorities and lived one step ahead of the law.

In his ministry, Father Miguel felt the closeness to Christ that our Lord himself had promised and that his disciples and ministers have experienced ever since. As he wrote:

> Here in the midst of the vortex I am amazed by the special aid of God, the very special graces he grants us in such perils, and *how his presence is now more intimately felt when discouragement comes* to make our souls smaller. I understand very well — and three times over — the cry of St. Paul, asking God to take him from this earth. But at the same time I feel the truth of the divine reply: "My grace is sufficient for thee; for my strength is made perfect in infirmity" (2 Cor. 12:9).[9]

In his afflictions and death, Father Miguel experienced the gift of fortitude, the divine virtue and strength promised to Christ's ministers in our infirmity. According to St. Thomas Aquinas, Father Miguel and Father de Padilla and all the martyrs down through the centuries are the true exemplars of the virtue of fortitude. In fact, we could say that for Thomas the martyrs are the ultimate Christian disciples, those who bear witness most perfectly to the love of God and the love of their neighbor.

In Thomas we see the culmination of what we have been looking at in this book — the transformation of the classical virtue of fortitude in light of the Word of God and the revelation of Jesus Christ. In holding up the martyrs, Thomas shows the radical way in which Christian fortitude differs from the fortitude of the philosophers. That radical difference is the person of Christ, who is the perfection of the virtues. As the moral philosopher, Rebecca Konyndyk De Young, has recognized:

> [Thomas's] choice to give the act of martyrdom precedence over the paradigm of military heroism as the exemplary act of courage, reflects his commitment to taking Christ — especially in his act of sacrificial love on the cross — as the model of virtue, thereby departing radically from alternative ideals of courage found in both ancient Greek and contemporary culture.[10]

The martyr most perfectly imitates the virtues of Jesus Christ. "Of all human actions," Thomas writes, "martyrdom is the most perfect kind, being the mark of the greatest love."[11] The martyr becomes the "ideal human being" in Thomas's Christian humanism. We have already seen this sensibility in the martyrs of the first Christian era. We recall the words of St. Ignatius of Antioch as he contemplated his martyrdom: "Once arrived there, *I shall be a man*. Permit me to be an *imitator* of my suffering God."[12]

The imitation of Christ, the suffering God, is the means by which we become truly human in the *imago Dei*. This imitation is most perfectly realized in the martyr's act of endurance. As we move into our study of courage in Thomas, we must keep in mind how his treatment of this virtue fits in with his overall vision of human transformation and growth in the *imago Christi*.

As we discussed in the last chapter, Thomas advances a true Christian humanism that gives us a beautiful template for understanding our lives. He has a dynamic understanding that the human person is created in the *imago Dei* and called to life-long conversion and transformation — *in Christ* and *in imitation of Christ*, who is the perfect image of God and the perfect image of man. This transformation is made possible by the gift of God's grace. With this gift we are able to become progressively more like God by growing in our likeness to Christ, as we make our way back to the Father and to the blessedness of divine communion for which we were created. As Dominican Archbishop J. Augustine Di Noia has written:

> Perhaps less widely known is how thoroughly christological and eschatological is the theology of the *imago Dei* advanced in the writings of St. Thomas Aquinas.... Aquinas's expansive treatise on the moral life unfolds as an explication of what it means for man to be made in the image of God. Here the dynamic character of the *imago Dei* is clear: human beings must be active in the grace-enabled actualization of the image of God within them. Coming from God, they are participants in the movement of their return to him. What draws them is their pursuit of the good of human life which is continually revealed as the good beyond life.... Aquinas can be construed as advancing a theology of the *imago Dei* that shows how, in the gracious plan of divine Providence, religious perfection is central to human and moral fulfillment. The human person is created in the image of God in order to grow into the image of Christ.[13]

Thomas's treatise on the virtue of fortitude in his *Summa Theologiae* is the most systematic in all of early Christian and medieval philosophy. And what makes Thomas's treatment so distinctive is his unique understanding of the person and work of Jesus Christ, who is both model and the cause of fortitude in us. In reading this treatise, one can be struck by his learned and creative use of classical authors, especially Aristotle and his *Nichomachean Ethics*. But Domincan Father Romanus Cessario rightly calls attention to what we can easily overlook — namely, that "the major influence in the treatise derives from his meditation on the passion of Christ and the witness of the Christian martyrs."[14] As we will see, this influence is even more pronounced when we consider Thomas's discussion of the virtue in his other works, especially in his commentaries on sacred Scripture.

The Passion of Christ and the Identity of the Priest

The image of Christ's passion in Thomas is of particular importance for priests and men preparing for the priesthood. His image of Christ as the perfect priest and the perfect man of virtue offers many inspiring insights for the man who is called to serve *in persona Christi*. Unfortunately, it is beyond my scope to talk much here about Thomas's teaching on the priesthood. But it is important to point out a few things.

First, Christ's "priesthood" is central to Thomas's understanding of Christ's identity and the purposes of his incarnation. Thomas sees Christ's work of redemption as priestly and liturgical. Through his passion and death on the cross, in which he offers himself humbly in sacrifice out of love for God and love for us, Jesus made an act of true and perfect worship to God. By this priestly act, Jesus atoned for the sin of the world, which had made the whole human race enemies of God; he reconciled man with God and made it possible for us to once more share in the divine life, which was God's intention in creating us in the beginning.[15]

This whole redemptive work Thomas describes in priestly terms. He understands the office of priest primarily as being "a mediator between God and the people." Noting that the Latin word for priest, *sacerdos,* means "one who gives holy things," Thomas observes that the priest in the Old Testament brings people the Law of God through his teaching; in addition, through his offering of sacrifices and prayers, the Old Testament priest "in some degree makes reparation to God for their sins."[16] Thomas concludes:

> Now these functions are carried out by Christ in an eminent degree. For through him divine gifts are brought to men. "By whom [Christ] he hath given us most great and precious promises: that by these you may be made partakers of the divine nature" (2 Pet. 1:4). It was he also who reconciled the human race to God. "In him [Christ] it hath well pleased the Father that all fullness should dwell, and through him to reconcile all things unto himself" (Col. 1:19–20). Consequently, Christ was a priest in the fullest sense of the word.[17]

The priest is a mediator between God and his people. Through his teaching and offering of sacrifices, he communicates to people the gifts of God revealed by Christ. The most precious of these is the gift of participation in the divine life through the grace conferred by the sacraments of the Church. This brings us to the second point I want to make about Thomas's teaching on the priesthood. Christ's redemptive work, accomplished in his passion and death, is proclaimed and continued in the Church, through the sacraments. For Thomas, the sacraments are always "the sacraments *of the Church.*" Cardinal Yves Congar has explained that for Thomas, the Church is "the sacrament of the cross, the sacrament of the unique mediatorship of Christ crucified ... the sacrament, the effective sign, and giver of the gift of new life and union of men in Christ their Savior."[18]

The Church is a sacrament and it exists for the sacraments — to communicate the life-giving fruits of the cross through its sacramental and liturgical ministry. By his passion, "by offering himself as 'an oblation and a sacrifice to God,'"[19] Christ inaugurated the sacramental liturgy of the Church. This, for Thomas, is symbolized by the water and blood that flowed out of Christ's side as he hung on the cross; these were symbols of baptism and the Eucharist.[20]

This is symbolic, too, of the priestly and liturgical character of the crucifixion. Thus, Thomas can say both that "the whole liturgy of the Christian religion is derived from Christ's priesthood,"[21] and again that "the sacraments of the Church derive their power specially from Christ's passion."[22] In the sacraments, all the faithful share in the benefits of Christ's priesthood.[23] "Christ's passion is, so to say, applied to man through the sacraments," according to Thomas.[24]

The sacraments make us holy,[25] by grace conferring on us the virtues and the gifts of the Holy Spirit.[26] The sacraments are the "means by which man wins the kingdom" promised by Christ.[27] By the sacraments we are deified — given the new, divine life won for us by Christ's passion. For, as Thomas notes, quoting 2 Peter 1:4, "grace is nothing else but a participated likeness of the divine nature."[28]

It follows, then, that in the divine economy of salvation, "God's ministers," his priests, play a special role. Through the sacrament of Holy Orders, a man is consecrated, "deputed to a spiritual service pertaining to the worship of God ... deputed to acts becoming the Church."[29] This is the third point I want to make. The priest, for Thomas, is a man for others. As the sacraments are always *of the Church*, so the priest is always described by Thomas as a *minister of the Church*.

This ecclesial self-understanding of the priest — the priest as a man who exists *from* and *for* the Church — is something that needs to be recovered in our day. As Thomas teaches, the Church, which is the body of Christ, is the authority and reason for the priestly ministry. In the Church, only the priest is ordained to confer the sacraments on others. As Christ was in his earthly ministry, the priest is "the appointed intermediary between God and the people."[30] He communicates the holy things of Christ by the divine power given to him in ordination.

"Christ is the fountain-head of the entire priesthood,"[31] according to Thomas. And ordination confers upon the priest "the character of Christ" and a participation in Christ's own priesthood.[32] As Christ's priesthood was ordered to the sacrifice of the cross, the powers conferred upon the priest are ordered to the Eucharist, which is "the sacrifice of the Church,"[33] and which contains "the whole mystery of our salvation."[34]

When we say that the priest should have an ecclesial self-understanding, an understanding of himself as a man *of the Church*, we are really saying that the priest should understand himself to be *a man of the Eucharist*. As shepherds of the Church, the priest is entrusted with responsibility for the Church which, as Thomas says, "God ... himself built ... with his blood."[35]

In the Church, built upon the blood of the cross, the priest is given a certain "likeness" to God because God established the priesthood to deliver his very life to his people through the sacraments. As a result, Thomas can say that priests are "made like God in their own way, as cooperating with God."[36]

The Eucharist is the source and the summit of the sacraments. As baptism begins the believer's new divine life in the Spirit, the Eucharist is "the consummation" of this spiritual life and "the end of all the sacraments."[37] Thus, there is an intensely eucharistic quality to the priest's identity, according to Thomas. Holy Orders is "directed to the sacrament of the Eucharist chiefly, and to the other sacraments consequently, for even the other sacraments flow from that which is contained in that sacrament."[38] To put it more directly: for Thomas, the Eucharist is the reason for the Church, and the reason for the priest's ministry.

> A priest has two acts: one is the principal, namely to consecrate the body of Christ; the other is secondary, namely to prepare God's people for the reception of this sacrament.[39]

This is a good way for the priest to understand his mission — as centered on the Eucharist. All that he does — his teaching, his ministry in the confessional, his preaching, his administrative duties, his work in the community — is ordered to preparation, to getting God's people ready for the encounter with the Jesus Christ in the Eucharist.

According to the teaching of St. Thomas, then, the powers of the priest are immense and extraordinary. The priest inherits the apostolic authority. He holds the "power of the keys" — the power to open the doors to eternal life through the sacraments.[40] The priest prepares and brings people into a true encounter with Jesus Christ who, through the priest's ministry, bestows on people the "life of grace."[41]

Following the teaching of the New Testament, Thomas understands that the priest does nothing of his own power. He is merely a representative, a sacrament, an effective sign of the only real power in the universe, the power of God. "A minister is a kind of instrument," a means by which God bestows his divine gifts upon his people, says Thomas.[42]

Thomas makes a comparison between the priest's powers and those given to the apostles. "Power was given to the apostles, not that they themselves might heal the sick, but that the sick might be healed at the prayer of the apostles."[43] In the same way, power is given to the priest, not so that he himself might bring divine life to people, but that divine life might be given to them through the agency of his priestly prayer, his sacramental ministry.

This is the fourth and final observation I want to make about Thomas's teaching on the priesthood. The priest is a man of the Church and a man of the Eucharist, sharing in an intimate way in God's plan for the salvation and blessing of his creation. In this, the priest participates in the priesthood of Jesus Christ. This participation defines, not only the functions that the priest performs, but his very character and identity.

For Thomas, the sacrament of Orders imprints upon the man a new Christ-like character.[44] The man is configured *to be Christ* for the people he ministers to. This identity is shaped by the power given to him to consecrate the Eucharist, which "contains within itself Christ in whom there is not only the character but the very plentitude of priesthood."[45]

The priest by his ordination shares the rank of the apostles, to whom Christ entrusted authority and power at the Last Supper. As such, the priest alone, acting "in the person of Christ" is empowered to consecrate the Eucharist.[46] Again, it is important to stress that for Thomas the priest "consecrates... not by his own power, but as the minister of Christ in whose person he consecrates."[47]

The priest "bears Christ's image" in his sacramental ministry.[48] This is true also in his ministry in the confessional. In the sacrament of penance, "the priest, by deed and word... signifies the work of God who forgives sins."[49] Once more, we see that in this sacrament the priest serves as an instrument of

God's own power.[50] Especially in penance and the Eucharist, the priest functions in such a way that it is "as if Christ were speaking in person."[51]

I have only skimmed the surface of Aquinas's teaching on the priestly ministry, and only to emphasize how our priesthood flows from the priesthood of Christ in his passion and death on the cross. That means the priest must take Jesus Christ as much more than a role model for his ministry, although Christ should be that for us, too. Our imitation of Christ must be more than surface. It must be intimate and integral. It must reach into the core of our understanding of ourselves as priests and ministers of God. Our lives must bear witness to a courageous, ever deepening configuration to the priesthood of Jesus Christ.

I must here repeat something I have tried to emphasize throughout this book: the priestly vocation is a thrilling participation in the holiness and mission of the Trinity. But the priest is not called to be a perfect man. The sacramental identity that we receive in Orders does not cancel out our faults and weaknesses. The power to act *in persona Christi* is instrumental, not actual. We are vessels for God's power. In the negative sense, this means, as the Church has always believed, that we can do the work of God whether we are holy or not.

However, we are called *and capable in Christ* of so much more than mediocrity. The priest is called to desire the perfection and holiness of Christ and to strive, with the help of God's grace, to achieve some measure of that perfection and holiness in his life. We are not perfect, but we should want to be — for Christ and for the people we serve. And in this we must turn to our model, Jesus Christ.

Every Action of Christ Is for Our Instruction

Thomas often said that "every action of Christ is for our instruction."[52] He begins the final part of his *Summa Theologiae* with the statement that Jesus Christ "showed us in his own person the way of truth."[53] This gives a distinct christological cast to Thomas's moral teaching. Christ becomes the example of virtuous conduct, a pattern for our own lives and our growth in virtue. Again, to quote Cardinal Congar: "He [Christ] is set up as our exemplar and pattern — to be contemplated as the measure and standard of our fashioning, becoming like unto him in the movement of our return towards God."[54]

Thomas's notion of the *imitatio Christi* is based on his deep understanding of what God was doing in sending his only Son into the world.

> Christ assumed human nature in order to restore fallen humanity. He had therefore to suffer and do, according to human nature, the things which could serve as a remedy against the sin of the fall. Man's sin consists in this — that he so cleaves to bodily goods that he neglects what is good spiritually.
>
> It was therefore necessary for the Son of God to show this in the humanity he had taken, through all he did and suffered, so that men should repute temporal things, whether good or evil, as nothing; for otherwise, hindered by an exaggerated affection for them, they would be less devoted to spiritual things.
>
> Christ therefore chose poor people for his parents — people nevertheless perfect in virtue, so that none of us should glory in the mere rank or wealth of our parents. He led the life of a poor man, to teach us to set no store by wealth. He lived the life of an ordinary man, without any rank, to wean men from an undue desire for honors.

Toil, thirst, hunger, the aches of the body — all these he endured to encourage men, whom pleasures and delights attract, not to be deterred from virtue by the austerity a good life entails.

He went so far as to endure even death, lest the fear of death might at any time tempt man to abandon the truth. And lest any of us might dread to die even a shameful death for the truth, he chose to die by the most accursed death of all, by crucifixion.

That the Son of God, made man, should suffer death was also fitting for this reason — that by his example he stimulates our courage, and so makes true what St. Peter said, "Christ suffered for us leaving you an example that you should follow his steps" (1 Pet. 2:21).[55]

Let us try to unpack this concise yet profound statement. Thomas describes the sin of the human race as a forgetfulness of man's spiritual purpose and eternal destiny. Instead, we become mired in the things of the flesh, the pleasures and concerns of this temporal world, and cannot find our way back to God.

The Son of God came in the flesh to teach us how to move from the life of the flesh to the life of the Spirit, from a life that finds its focus and meaning in the affections of this world to a spiritual life aimed at the virtues, holiness, and beatitude. According to Thomas: "Therefore divine Wisdom, who had made man, took to himself a bodily nature and visited man immersed in things of the body, so that by the mysteries of his bodily life he might recall man to spiritual life."[56]

In his humanity, in his bodily life, Christ recalls to us our spiritual purpose. In Christ, we see how our earthly reality should be ordered to our supernatural destiny. This does not mean a rejection of the good things of this world, but rather a proper ordering of them and a detachment from exaggerated affection for material things, honors, and wealth.

That is why Jesus comes among us in signs of poverty and humility. "Christ chose everything that was rejected and low in the world," Thomas taught.[57] He does that to show us that the ordinary means of earthly prestige and power are unimportant to the life of virtue and holiness for which we are created. This is also why Christ shared in all the weaknesses and infirmities of the human condition — again, to show us that affliction and hardship should not be an obstacle in our pursuit of the spiritual life.

We note, finally, that Thomas singles out "fear of death" as a crucial obstacle to our growth in this spiritual life. He also holds up Christ in his passion as a model for our own "courage" in the face of hardships. As we will see, this is a note that Thomas sounds again and again in his writing.

Jesus Christ is the model of the virtues because "in Christ... all virtues and graces and gifts are found superabundantly." He is the Messiah that the prophet Isaiah promised would be filled with grace and the Spirit, including the spirit of fortitude.[58] As perfect man, Jesus possessed the perfection of the virtues. "He is... called a man because of the perfection of all the virtues that were in him."[59] Throughout his life, as recorded in the gospels, Christ gave his followers examples of virtuous behavior.[60]

In Thomas's scheme of *imitatio Christi*, a special place is reserved for the cross.

> For the passion of Christ completely suffices to fashion our lives. Whoever wishes to live perfectly should do nothing but disdain what Christ disdained on the cross, and desire what he desired. For the cross exemplifies every virtue.[61]

Thomas frequently quotes St. Augustine, who said that the cross was both an altar upon which Christ suffered and a seat from which he taught.[62] Christ's death on the cross is both "a sacrament of salvation" and "an example of perfect virtue for us."[63]

The Scourge of Fear in the Priestly Life

Of all the virtues demonstrated in their human perfection on the cross, the virtue that Thomas cites the most is that of fortitude.

> By his death Christ also gave an example of *fortitude*, which does not abandon justice in the face of adversity. Refusal to give up the practice of virtue even under fear of death seems to pertain most emphatically to fortitude.... In not refusing to die for truth, Christ overcame *the fear of dying, which is the reason men for the most part are subject to the slavery of sin.*[64]

Again we note Thomas's keen attention to the "fear of death" as the root cause of our subjection to sin. We will return to that in a moment. Here it is important to point out that Christ's passion and death are far more than a moral model for us as believers. As we have already discussed, the passion of Christ and the merits of his sufferings opened up the gates of heaven and made possible our participation in the divine life — through "the inpouring of grace" and the fullness of the virtues in the sacraments.[65] In baptism, we are infused by the Holy Spirit with the theological virtues of faith, hope, and charity, along with the moral virtues of prudence, justice, fortitude, and temperance. We also receive the corresponding seven gifts of the Holy Spirit — fear, fortitude, piety, counsel, knowledge, understanding, and wisdom.

The newness of life we receive in baptism, then, includes both the *infused virtue* of fortitude and the *spiritual gift* of fortitude. And in Thomas's reckoning, fortitude is essential to a healthy spiritual life: "In a good life, prudence is like the eye, which directs a person; and courage is like the feet, which support and carry him."[66] As our feet support us and make it possible for us to walk and move from one place to another, our life in the Spirit is upheld and enabled by the virtue of fortitude. We could not stand without fortitude, nor could we make progress in the spiritual life without this virtue.

In the early pages of his treatise in the *Summa*, Thomas quotes those inspiring words of St. Ambrose: "Courage ... defends the glories and protects the decisions of all the virtues. It wages relentless war against all the vices — unbowed by toil, brave in the face of danger, even more unbending in the face of pleasures."[67] Thomas agrees that fortitude involves a steadfast and unwavering resistance in the face of vices and other conditions hostile to the moral life. Yet Thomas focuses his attention on fortitude as the virtue that combats our fears, and the root of all those fears, the fear of death.

His analysis is especially important for pastors of souls. Fear is a great scourge in the Christian life, and it can be a real problem in the apostolate of the priest. Not long before his death, Pope John Paul II published his final book, and fittingly, the final section is a meditation on "God and Courage." In it he cites the words of his mentor, Cardinal Stefan Wyszyński:

> The greatest weakness in an apostle is fear. What gives
> rise to fear is *lack of confidence in the power of the Lord*; this
> is what oppresses the heart and tightens the throat. The
> apostle then ceases to offer witness.[68]

In every time and place, the priest is called to be a sign of contradiction. This is especially true in the cultural climate of the modern world, which has become aggressively secular and materialistic. This cultural condition has many implications for priestly ministry. The philosopher Charles Taylor has described our cultural situation as one of "exclusive humanism."[69] In essence, he argues that societies in the West are built on Enlightenment prejudices that see organized religion and Church doctrine as barriers to human freedom and development. These deep-seated prejudices are behind the intense pressures to exclude all talk of God, faith, and religious values from public life in the West.

As a result, in my view, "practical atheism" has almost become the *de facto* state religion in America and throughout the West. By this I mean that more and more, in order to live in our society, to participate in its economic and political life, people are required to conduct themselves as if God does not exist.

In this hostile climate the priest, no different than other believers, faces dangers — on both the levels of personal spirituality and public witness. In his spiritual life, under the relentless and corrosive proselytizing of a secular and materialistic culture, he may be tempted to question the wisdom or continued relevance of certain Church teachings. He may be tempted to make concessions or compromises in his ascetical life, to quietly loosen or even abandon certain standards of discipline, habits of life, and pious practices intended to foster his virtue and strengthen the effectiveness of his ministry.

On the level of proclamation and witness, similar doubts can creep in, along with similar temptations. In the pulpit, in the confessional, in his various roles in the wider civic community, the priest can be tempted to downplay, "water down," and even ignore the truths of the Gospel and the demands of the Church's moral teachings. Sometimes these temptations to compromise can come from a misguided sense of prudence. Most often, however, I would say that the problems stem, quite simply, from *fear* — fear of undertaking difficult or risky tasks;

fear of attracting criticism or displeasure, fear of unwanted outcomes.

Much of pastoral timidity is rooted in undue concern for "human respect" — concern that we not "embarrass" ourselves, or lose our moral influence and standing with our people or the wider community by coming off as too strident or too "dogmatic." This can be a legitimate concern. But it can never be allowed to excuse silence or complacency or to justify the refusal to uphold the standards and teachings of the Church.

The Gospel we are called to proclaim is a call, not to accommodation, but to conversion. And the priest must proclaim that Gospel by his word and example, boldly and creatively. Our Lord demands nothing less. In the words of St. Paul, the priest must "preach the word, be urgent in season and out of season, convince, rebuke, and exhort; be unfailing in patience and in teaching."[70]

The question, then, becomes how and with what resources will the priest carry out his mission. The priest must find a reasonable mean between, on the one hand, the vice of timidity or cowardice, and on the other, the opposite vice of fearlessness or excessive daring, what Thomas calls, respectively, *intimiditatis* and *audacia*.[71]

If timidity can make us excessively fearful and overly cautious in the face of opposition and evil, fearlessness and daring can cause us to act impetuously, with a reckless, devil-may-care attitude and without regard to the dangers involved or the consequences of our actions. Sometimes, this excessive "fearlessness" can be the product of presumption and pride, a feeling that we can do no wrong because of our own intelligence and strength or because "God is on our side."

Spiritual Bravery: Fortitude in Thomas Aquinas

The infused virtue of fortitude helps the priest to resist both extremes. "Fortitude is about fear and daring — as curbing fear and moderating daring," Thomas writes.[72] If we recall our overview of Thomas's moral psychology in the previous chapter, the cardinal virtues moderate our passions and appetites and the workings of our will so that we conform to reason, which is ordered to our pursuit of the goods of the spiritual life. Thus, Thomas can say that "the task of the virtue of courage is to remove hindrance which holds back the will from following reason."[73] While it manifests itself in outward acts of bravery, courage is a steadfastness, a strength of the soul or the mind.[74] It is well described by Father Cessario as a form of "spiritual bravery."[75]

St. Thomas is a moral realist. He recognizes that in our pursuit of holiness and the call of the Father that comes to us in the Gospel, we will face difficulties, injustices, grave dangers, and other evils. Sometimes the obstacles we face will require us to attack and overcome them. Other times, we will be required to endure and persevere in the face of afflictions and difficulties. These are the principal acts of fortitude — *resistance* and *endurance*.

> The virtue of courage has the task of protecting the human will so that it is not turned back through fear of bodily harm from the good proposed by reason. Now we must hold steadfastly, in the face of any evil whatsoever, to the good proposed by reason, with which no mere bodily good can compare. Therefore courage of soul (*fortitude animi*) means the sort of courage which steadfastly, in the face of the greatest evils, preserves the attachment of the human will to the good prescribed by reason. For he who stands firm against greater evils naturally stands firm also against the lesser, though the converse is not true.

Furthermore, a virtue by its nature always presses to its own utmost objective. Now *the most dreaded of all bodily ills is death*, which removes all bodily good.... Therefore the virtue of courage is concerned with the fears associated with dangers of death.[76]

Fortitude fights fear. In Thomas's rich psychology, he identifies fear as the root stumbling block to our accomplishment of the good that God would have us pursue. Fear is a passion of the soul by which we imagine a future evil that seems beyond our powers of resistance.[77] Thomas recognizes that "fears of difficulties" often "cause the will to retreat from following the lead of reason."[78]

And the greatest of all fears that we experience is the fear of death. For Thomas, it would seem, all the lesser fears we experience are rooted in that chief fear (*timor praecipuus*) — the fear of death.[79] Thomas, again, is a realist. And for him, fear of death is the most "natural," even instinctive of human concerns. "Now it is natural to love one's own life. Therefore there must be a special virtue to govern fears of death."[80]

In this, Thomas agrees with Aristotle and most of classical philosophy.[81] But Thomas goes far beyond his philosophical influences in considering the implications of the fear of death both morally and theologically. The passage from the letter to the Hebrews that we considered in Chapter 5 is crucial to Thomas's understanding.

… that through death he [Christ] might destroy him who has the power of death, that is, the devil, and deliver all those who through fear of death were subject to lifelong bondage.[82]

Following Hebrews, Thomas presents the fear of death as "the reason men for the most part are subject to the slavery of sin."[83] Again, Thomas is a realist, not a fundamentalist. And it is the reality of our moral lives that confirms for him this truth of Scripture. How often fear causes us to abandon our convictions or fail to do what we ought.

Thomas speaks as a wise observer of souls when he writes: "It is fear of mortal danger which is most powerful to cause a person to draw back from reason's good."[84] This is natural, because, "as man loves his life above all things, so does he fly from dangers of death more than any others."[85]

What I would add is that there are countless "lesser" fears that draw us back from the good — fears of difficulties, fears of the opinion of others, fears of being misunderstood, fears of losing friendships or influence. These fears are in some way rooted in that primal fear of "mortal danger." They are, in a way, fears of certain kinds of "death," for instance, the "death" of one's reputation or prestige. Thomas seems to recognize this, too.

Thomas agrees with Aristotle that there is not necessarily any virtue in being brave in the face of a robbery, or storms at sea, or sickness. In order to be an expression of true courage, the believer must be facing danger or death "through his pursuing of some good."[86] And while he agrees that certainly a soldier in a just war is courageous in the pursuit of the good, Thomas wants to open up wide new paths for understanding courage.

He says that, in addition to general combat in war, there is all manner of *"private combat,"* or individual confrontations related to one's pursuit of the good. It is significant that the one example Thomas chooses is a case of courage in the defense of one's *conscience* — "for example, when a judge or even a private individual refuses to be moved from a just decision by fear of a brandished sword or any peril whatsoever, even mortal."[87]

For Thomas, enduring a brandished sword or a death threat would not be "praiseworthy in itself — but only insofar as it is directed towards some good consisting in an act of virtue, such as *faith* or *the love of God.*[88] Courage, then, is not only to be found on the battlefield where men pursue patriotic goals. A courageous man is also one who is willing to suffer in defense of what is just and right. A courageous man is one who suffers for the love of God and the truths of faith.

Thomas gives two more examples that are expressly drawn from the experience of Christian charity and missionary work. He calls courageous the man who "does not shrink from attendance on a sick friend for fear of deadly infection." He also gives the example of one who "does not shrink from a journey with some godly object (*ad aliquod pium*) because of fear of shipwreck or bandits."[89]

For classical thinkers, the "good of one's country" was the "preeminent human good" (*bonum reipublicae est praecipuum inter bona human*). But for Thomas there is a higher good — the "divine good," which is "superior to any human good" (*bonum divinum... est potius quam humanum*).

Here, Thomas makes the decisive turn. He recognizes that a human good can be made a divine good if one makes it his intention to seek this good for the love of God.

> Yet, since any human good can become divine, for instance when directed to God, any human good can become a reason for martyrdom, inasmuch as it is directed to God.[90]

Thomas opens the door to a wider understanding of martyrdom and of the virtue that enables and sustains the martyr's witness. Fortitude takes on a vastly more expansive profile. No longer do we find courageous men only among those willing to die on the battlefield. Examples of fortitude can be seen in the woman who, despite the pressures of society and even family, refuses to abort her unborn child; or the man who refuses to deny his principles even when promised the rewards of "freedom" or an "easy career."

Fortitude, as Pope John Paul II has said, enables the Christian in many ordinary circumstances of daily living to "'go beyond' his own limits and 'transcend' himself, running 'the risk' of an unknown situation, the risk of being frowned upon, the risk of laying himself open to unpleasant consequences, insults, degradations, material losses, perhaps imprisonment or persecution."[91]

Fortitude becomes the virtue of the servant of Christ in all walks of life, who is committed to the love of God, the *bonum divinum*. By fortitude we can be firm in the face of difficulty and constant in our pursuit of the good. By fortitude we are strengthened in all the private combats of our spiritual lives — enabled to "resist temptations and to overcome obstacles in the moral life."[92]

Thomas thus transforms the virtue from one focused on human power, initiative, and control, to one of divine strength given as a gift of a loving Father to his children, that we might grow in likeness to him. As Konyndyk De Young concludes:

> By modeling courage on the example of Christ's own suffering and steadfast witness, Aquinas directs our moral gaze beyond the limits of human life and power to a life in which virtue and happiness are perfected by a power that is both beyond us and yet can become our own.[93]

Jesus Christ, Root and Source of Our Strength

We see in Thomas, finally, the water of classical moral philosophy changed into the wine of Gospel wisdom.[94] Thomas takes the vision and insight of the Christian Fathers to greater depths. St. Augustine had recognized that "fortitude is love ready to bear all things for God's sake."[95] But in Thomas that recognition is wed to a deep moral psychology and a theological understanding of Christ as both the exemplar and the true *source* of courage. Christ is "the foundation and the roots … the source of [our] strength," as Thomas sees it.[96]

In his biblical commentaries, Thomas takes care to notice how often Christ is shown dispelling fears and "strengthening" his disciples.[97] The lesson he draws from this is that "God will strengthen you, because God is faithful. God would not seem to be faithful, if he called us to the fellowship of his Son and then denied us on his part the things by which we could attain to him."[98]

For the priest, this is a most reassuring teaching — that God who has called us to the service of his people will give us the strength and the courage we need to fulfill our calling. Thomas gives us confidence that Christ will always be with those who love them — that he will give them the gift of his own strength.

He interprets the petition in the Lord's Prayer for "daily bread" as a confident appeal for this divine assistance and power.

> This gift of fortitude prevents man's heart from fainting through fear of lacking necessities, and makes him trust without wavering that God will provide him whatever he needs. For this reason the Holy Spirit, the giver of this fortitude, teaches us to pray to God to *give us this day our daily bread.* For this reason, he is called "the Spirit of Fortitude" (Isa. 11:2).[99]

This is the beauty of Thomas's teaching on the infused virtues and the gifts of the Holy Spirit. We are not left to our own devices in our calling to serve him. The struggles we face, we do not have to face with our own powers alone. The One who has called us to his service will strengthen us. And he has poured the gifts of his strength into us at baptism.

By the infusion of the virtue of fortitude we are able to courageously bear witness to his Gospel and overcome all that would thwart us in our ministries. We are given "a steadfastness of mind towards all hostile elements," and the power to "resist the attacks of all the vices."[100]

By the infusion of the virtue of fortitude, we can be *magnanimous* — that is, we can aspire to do great things in our priestly ministry solely for the love and honor of God.[101] We can be *magnificent* — that is, we can attempt and perform great works through our hard work and the generous expenditure of our gifts and resources.[102] With fortitude, we can resist the vices that would cause us to stumble in our courageous efforts.

Fortitude helps us to fight *presumption*, which would have us believe that by our own powers, and "without trust in God's help," we can perform the ministry that has been entrusted to us.[103] Fortitude, too, helps us to resist the sin of *ambition*, by which we are tempted to seek human respect or higher office in the Church as a kind of "prize" for our pastoral successes — forgetting that "man is not the source of his own excellence, rather it is a divine gift within him, so ... recognition is owed chiefly to God and not to the man."[104]

Vainglory is one of the "hidden enemies" in the priestly life,[105] because it causes us to seek to establish ourselves as the center of attention and authority, and not Christ and his Gospel. This can lead us to actions that are unseemly — such as boasting of our accomplishments or acting in ways that are hypocritical or divisive. But vainglory can also become scandalous, as it does when priests are led to substitute their own judgments for the sound wisdom and teaching of the Church — whether it be in the confessional, in the pulpit, or in the celebration of the liturgy. Fortitude helps us to resist this vice, and especially its manifestation in what Thomas calls the "passion for innovation" (*novitatum praesumptio*).

This restless desire to be celebrated for one's creativity and innovations — in moral teaching and in the liturgy especially — is arguably at the root of many problems in the post-Vatican II Church.

Finally, fortitude helps us to resist *pusillanimity*,[106] which would cause us to bury our talents for fear of failure or out of an unhealthy sense of our own inadequacy; and it helps us to resist the related vice of *pettiness*, which causes us to be stingy and unduly "calculating" in the giving of ourselves and our time, talent, and treasure.[107]

Thomas assigns the virtues of *magnanimity* and *magnificence* as parts of the cardinal virtue of fortitude. He also includes as parts of fortitude the virtues of *patience* and *perseverance*. The virtue of *patience*, which is a gift of God's grace, helps us to counter the sadness or dejection that inevitably afflicts us when we contemplate the evils and obstacles that face us in our ministry.[108] *Perseverance* is the virtue that empowers us to carry on resolutely in our cultivation of the virtues and in our service of God's will, despite these evils and obstacles.[109]

And in all our efforts in the Christian moral life, we are assisted by the gift of the Holy Spirit, known also as fortitude. Like the other gifts of the Spirit, the gift of fortitude is given to us in baptism and renewed in confirmation.[110] The purpose of the gift is to keep our souls awake to the promptings of the Spirit in the midst of all the distractions, temptations, and hardships of our ministries.

By this gift, the Spirit enables us to do what we otherwise could not do on our own — in our moral lives and in our proclamation of the Gospel. As Thomas says:

> Sometimes it does not lie within human power to attain the end of one's work, or to escape evils or dangers, since these sometimes press in upon us to the point of death.

But the Holy Spirit achieves this in us ... and he pours
into our minds a certain confidence.[111]

Fear Makes Cowards of Us All

Through the gifts and the infused virtues, we have the
spiritual foundation for our priestly ministries. We can and
must acquire and grow in the natural or acquired virtues. It
is essential that we develop good habits of virtuous living so
that our lives are regulated by reason and so that we promptly
perform and delight in the exercise of the virtues. The infusion
of the virtues and the gifts of the Spirit guarantee that all our
natural efforts may be "deified" or "supernaturalized" — elevated and transfigured — in order that we might accomplish
the mightier works that God sets before us.[112] What would be
impossible by our own natural strength is possible by Christ,
who is the source of our supernatural strength.

In the case of fortitude, the infused form of the virtue helps
us to govern our passions, to restrain our wills, and to order our
hearts and hands to the love of God and our neighbor. As the
Dominican spiritual master, Father John Arintero, has written:

> Natural fortitude, attentive to human appraisals, seeks
> to overcome certain difficulties which impede the ful-
> fillment of duty; Christian fortitude, without any other
> appraisal than that of the glory of God, enables one to
> perform the most difficult enterprises, and seeks thus to
> triumph over all enemies, even that enemy which dis-
> simulates most: self-love.[113]

In light of what we have already discussed about Thomas's
moral psychology, we might understand "self-love" — and by
extension all our greater and lesser dispositions and acts of selfishness — as expressing what Thomas identifies as the primal
fear of death. "Fear makes cowards of us all," Thomas tells us
bluntly but wisely. "Hence, if a man overcomes his fears, he

overcomes everything. And when fear is overcome, all disordered love of the world is overcome."[114]

All our disordered loves, Thomas seems to say, all our self-love, is rooted in our fear of death. The Dominican Father John J. McDonald has written: "Every sin, in a sense, is an act of cowardice, since in every sin there is an element of inordinate fear."[115] Here we glimpse in some measure the power of Christ's passion. For by his passion, Christ destroys the power of death, and with it the fear of death.

> Thus Christ, by His death, broke this fear, because he removed the fear of death, and, consequently the love of the present life. For when a person considers that the Son of God, the Lord of death, willed to die, he no longer fears death.[116]

Christ is the exemplar of the fortitude that Thomas envisions for the ministers of the Church. In his love of God, Jesus did not shrink from his mission, even in the face of opposition and threats of violence. In this, he overcame the most basic of human fears. And in this, he showed us the greatest of love, the love that enables a man to give up his very life. Again, Thomas explains:

> The strongest of human loves is the love with which a man loves himself. Therefore this love must be the measure, by comparison with which we estimate the love by which a man loves others than himself.... It is the greatest of all signs of love if a man is willing, by dying for his friend, to lay down his very life. Therefore, that Christ, in suffering laid down his life, was the greatest of all signs that he loved us.[117]

Fortitude, like the other virtues, is a means, not an end. It is a means for love which is the motive and the perfection of the virtues. This is the love that we are called to in our pastoral ministry *in persona Christi*. It is a love that manifests itself in vulnerability and weakness, that fears nothing for the sake of the beloved, Christ. In this love, made possible by grace and the gift of fortitude, we can imitate Jesus Christ, the man of perfect virtue and the man of fortitude. We can reproduce in our lives the life of Christ.

All our fears in our apostolic ministry are rooted in a lack of confidence in the power of God. Yet Christ in his love has overcome all that we fear and shown us the way to overcome our fears through hope in his resurrection. Thus, we too, in our ministries, can offer ourselves out of love for God and his will for his sons and daughters.

CHAPTER 8

His Heart Was Courageous in the Ways of the Lord

Forming Priests in the Virtue of Fortitude

THE LATE ARCHBISHOP LUIS M. MARTÍNEZ of Mexico City was a great preacher and writer and a courageous pastor. During the persecution in Mexico, he was a true peacemaker who saved many churches from destruction, and in the long, painful years that followed, he helped to foster a spirit of reconciliation in the country. In one of his last books, Archbishop Martínez wrote:

> Heaven belongs to the strong, and for this reason there are relatively few saints: for few have the fortitude to make the efforts and sacrifices required by perfection.[1]

At the end of our study of the Christian virtue of fortitude and its place in the moral and spiritual formation of priests, his words seem a fitting reminder of the goal, the "end" of all our priestly efforts. And that is to be saints and to help others become saints too. We are "called to be saints," as St. Paul said.[2] Our holiness comes in imitating the virtues of Christ and cultivating those virtues in our lives. To do this, we need to be strong. We need the divine strength of fortitude.

For priests the mission of the new evangelization is to help make new American saints, men and women seeking in everything they do to respond to the universal call to holiness. As Christ said it would be, this is a quiet process, invisible even — like the mustard seed, like the grain of wheat that dies in the ground in order to bear much fruit. "What is sown is perishable. What is raised is imperishable," St. Paul said.[3] St. Ambrose said: "The Church is beautiful in her saints."[4] And that is the joyful calling of priests in the new evangelization. We are here to make the Church beautiful by making saints. We are here to help turn men and women from what is perishable to what is imperishable.

In the preceding pages, we have talked about some of the saints, canonized and noncanonized, who sowed the seeds of the Gospel in the Americas and throughout the world. Through their sweat, blood, sacrifice, and prayer, the world has come to know Jesus. No one is a Catholic by chance. Everyone is able to know Jesus because of the witness of all those who went before them marked with the sign of faith. It is a great cloud of witnesses that extends back through the missionaries, all the way back to the apostles. This is the beauty of the communion of saints, the great extended family of the Church that stretches from earth to heaven, from the beginning of time to the end of history.

We know many of the saints by name. But most we will never know because they are unknown beyond the small circle of their families, their neighbors and coworkers, their fellow parishioners. And of the many heroic deeds performed by saints and blesseds, perhaps the most heroic is the quiet prayer and sacrifices they make, far from the crowds or public view. Pope Benedict XVI has quoted these words from Father Didimo Mantiero, a parish priest who lived in Bassano del Grappa, Italy:

> Converts have always been made through the prayer and sacrifice of unknown faithful. Christ won souls, not by the force of his marvelous words, but by the power of his constant prayer. He preached by day, but at night he prayed.[5]

This spirit of prayer and sacrifice in imitation of Christ characterized the short life of Frank Parater. By all accounts, Frank was an ordinary, devout young seminarian studying to be a priest for the Diocese of Richmond, Virginia. He had completed his regular seminary work, and his bishop had sent him for advanced study in philosophy and theology at the North American College in Rome. But while he was there, Frank contracted rheumatic fever. He died on February 7, 1920. Those who were at his bedside said his last act was to make the sign of the cross.

Among Frank's personal effects, his seminary rector discovered a sealed envelope marked, "My Last Will." It is an extraordinary document, so extraordinary that it was later published in the Vatican newspaper, *L'Osservatore Romano,* and Popes Benedict XV and Pius XI each requested personal copies of it. What is perhaps most remarkable is that it had been written more than a month before his death, when Frank was in perfect health.

> I have nothing to leave or give but my life, and this I have consecrated to the Sacred Heart of Jesus to be used as he wills. I have offered my all for the conversion to God of non-Catholics in Virginia. This is what I live for and, in the case of death, what I die for....
>
> Melancholic or morbid sentimentality is not the cause of my writing this, for I love life here, the college, the men, and Rome itself. But I have desired to die and be buried with the saints....
>
> Since I was a child, I have desired to die for the love of God and for my fellow man. Whether or not I shall receive that favor I know not, but if I live, it is for the same purpose; every action of my life here is offered to God for the spread and success of the Catholic Church in Virginia.[6]

In these words of humble prayer and self-offering, of serenity in the face of death, we see the heroic essence of the priesthood. Frank Parater's story reminds me of something the great Franciscan martyr St. Maximilian Kolbe used to say: *Spes messis in semine* — "The hope of the harvest is in the seed." He said this in reference to seminarians, reminding us that the word "seminary" means "seed-bed."[7]

The hope of the harvest of the new evangelization lies in the seeds of virtue we are able to help to sow in the hearts of our seminarians and priests. We need strong, courageous priests who want to serve God with their whole hearts, in imitation of Christ; strong men who have the desire and the courage to be saints. This was our purpose in beginning this study. In this final chapter I hope to bring together what we have been able to learn about the priestly vocation and the virtue of fortitude. Based on our study of the Scriptures, the ancient Church, and St. Thomas Aquinas, I hope now to be able to offer some practical suggestions for cultivating this virtue as part of an overall program of spiritual and moral formation centered on the *imitatio Christi*.

The Priesthood Was Invented by Love

To summarize what we have gleaned about the priesthood: The priest is the man of love. In a world darkened by self-seeking and the anxious avoidance of death, the priest is the apostle of love, a missionary sent by the God who reveals himself in the total gift of himself, the God who reveals himself to be a Love stronger than death.[8] The priesthood is the *amoris officium*, the office established by God to continue the work of his divine love.

Cardinal Emmanuel Suhard, the holy priest and archbishop of Paris, once said:

> The priesthood was invented by love.... Everything becomes clear in the priest. Others in the community have chosen glory, money, pleasure. Others devote their life to

knowing, giving orders, conquering. The priest has left
all. He has renounced all possessions; he has renounced
himself... *He has chosen love.* He wants it rather than all
the rest. He wants his brothers to be his sole possession.[9]

In these beautiful thoughts, we see the essence of the apostolic love that is the priesthood. "We have left everything
and followed you," St. Peter said on behalf of the Twelve.[10] The
apostolic love of the priest renounces the highest loves that this
world has to offer — the love of mother and father and brother
and sister; the love of wife and children — for the sake of an
even higher love, the highest love imaginable, the *bonum divinum*, the love of God.

The priest does not reject these other goods. He recognizes
them as precisely that — gifts of God's own love and goodness,
avenues of holiness and virtue in their own right. Rather than
follow these paths, the priest gives up these good things for a
higher love. He makes a sacrificial offering of himself and by
this sacrifice is able to offer himself freely and totally to Christ.
This is what it means to say that the *priest has chosen love.*

But the priest's choice is never his own initiative. His gift
of self is always a response, an answer to the divine calling, an
acceptance of the gift of *Christ's own choice.* This is the mystery
of election. "You did not choose me, but I chose you."[11] Of the
many who have been called to follow Christ, the priest is among
the few who are chosen personally by our Lord. The priest who
chooses love is first himself chosen in love. He has been appointed to participate in the mystery of God's plan of salvation.
He is chosen to be a "steward of the mysteries of God," an instrument of the "varied grace" and blessings that the Father seeks
to bestow upon his children in the sacraments of his Church.[12]

The greatness of Christ's priesthood can make us tremble.
We can be tempted to cry out with Peter: "Lord, depart

from me, for I am a sinful man" (Luke 5:8), because we find it hard to believe that Christ called us specifically. Could he not have chosen someone else, more capable, more holy?[13]

What priest cannot relate to the feelings Pope Benedict expresses here? Who among us ever feels really worthy of this calling? And yet we know, as the Pope continues, "Jesus has looked lovingly upon each one of us, and in this gaze of his we may have confidence."[14] The *confidence* that Benedict speaks of is what Pope John Paul II called "*the courage of the truth of our priesthood.*" The courage of this truth, the loving gaze of Christ, is the seal that has been placed upon us in ordination.

As bread and wine are transformed into the Body and Blood of Christ on the holy altar, a "wondrous exchange," an *admirabile commercium,* also takes place in ordination, says John Paul. He deliberately uses here a phrase the Church Fathers used to describe the incarnation. "A man offers his humanity to Christ, so that Christ may use him as an instrument of salvation, making him, as it were, another Christ." Thus, the Pope adds, "the priesthood, in its deepest reality, is the priesthood of Christ."[15]

Jesus has chosen to exercise his own priesthood in us. Our priesthood is a participation in Christ's own offering of his life, his Body and Blood, in a sacrifice of praise to the Almighty God, the Creator of heaven and earth. Thus, the Eucharist is the source and summit of our priesthood, the *sacramentum caritatis,* the sign and instrument of God's love. This is why St. Thomas Aquinas said the priest has only two acts — to consecrate the Body and Blood of Christ and to prepare people to receive this sacrament.[16]

There is a cosmic dimension to our priesthood that we must never forget. As Pope Benedict has said: "The ultimate end of all New Testament liturgy and of all priestly ministry is to make the world a temple and a sacrificial offering for God. This is to bring about the inclusion of the whole world into the Body of Christ, so that God may be all in all."[17]

This is what we do in offering the Mass every day. In this, the priest assumes an irreplaceable role in God's plan for the human race. We participate in the reconciliation of all things in heaven and on earth that Christ made by the blood of his cross.[18] The history of this reconciliation is well summarized in Eucharistic Prayer IV:

> Father ... you formed man in your own likeness
> and set him over the whole world to serve you, his
>   Creator....
> Even when he disobeyed you and lost your friendship
> you did not abandon him to the power of death....
> Again and again you offered a covenant to man, and...
> in the fullness of time you sent your only Son....
> In fulfillment of your will, he gave himself up to death,
> but by rising from the dead,
> he destroyed death and restored life...
> that we might live no longer for ourselves but for him.

Made in the *imago Dei*, the human race owes a debt of praise and thanksgiving to its Creator. We are called to live, not for ourselves but for him; to offer all of ourselves, the fruits of creation and the work of our hands, to God. Yet imprisoned in our disobedience, selfishness, and sin, captive to the fear of death, we were unable.

Christ, in his passion, death, and resurrection, broke the bonds of sin and set humanity free to serve him without fear. The Eucharist, the memorial of this act of love and redemption, becomes the perfect offering that humanity can make, a worship in which we make ourselves a living sacrifice and join our offering of ourselves to Christ's own self-offering; and in this liturgy that unites heaven and earth, God fills us with all the blessings of his love.[19]

The Daily Pressure of Anxiety for the Church

It is true: the greatness of Christ's priesthood should make us tremble. The priest stands as "the official mediator between heaven and earth," said Blessed Columba Marmion. "It is the privilege of the priesthood to ensure the return of creation in its entirety to the Master of all things."[20] But if this is true, we might ask, why does so much of what the priest does, day-to-day, seem so far from this lofty calling? In fact, much of the priest's ministry can seem downright mundane.

It is always important to remember that the mundane struggles the priest faces today have been with the Church's pastors since the beginning. Recall the words of Bishop Machebeuf that we quoted in our first chapter. Pastors have always been called to be, as he put it, "a little of everything" — functioning in some ways as managers of a small business, responsible for staff and programs, finances and operations, building maintenance, and more.

We have only to read the Acts of the Apostles or Paul's letters to the Corinthians to be reminded that pastors have always been stretched too thin and worked too hard; they have always had to fight to balance the spiritual and temporal needs of the Church and their own ministries; they have always had to deal with parochialism and factionalism in their congregations, divisions between young and old, rich and poor, progressive and conservative. The New Testament also testifies that pastors have always had to deal with believers whose understanding of the faith and the Eucharist could be superficial and compromised by the "different gospels"[21] found in the culture around them.

After listing all the sufferings he endured for the Gospel —
beatings, stonings, imprisonments, hunger and thirst and sleep-
less nights — Paul said something every pastor can understand:
"And apart from these other things there is *the daily pressure upon
me of my anxiety for all the churches.*"[22]

None of this mundane anxiety canceled out, for Paul or the
apostles or any of the great missionaries, the grand spiritual
mission of the priesthood as the ministry by which God rec-
onciles all things to himself in Christ. Nor can we in our day
allow ourselves to be overwhelmed by the burdens of administration and the other tedium of priestly life.

We must remember, as Pope Benedict has said, "The faithful expect only one thing from priests: that they be specialists
in promoting the encounter between man and God. The priest
is not asked to be an expert in economics, construction, or poli-
tics. He is expected to be an expert in the spiritual life."[23] On a
practical level, this will mean learning to delegate and to work
with others in order to express the clear priority of the spiritual
in our ministries.

But if the anxiety and pressures that pastors experience today are hardly new in the Church, this just underlines the point
I have been trying to make in this book — that the priests today, called to be the advance guard of the new evangelization,
have a tremendous need to grow in the virtue of fortitude, as
the centerpiece of a life of ongoing spiritual formation in the
virtues.

St. Augustine recognized in the fourth century that the
"ministers of the divine sacraments" face far greater difficulties
in maintaining the life of virtue to which all Christians are
called. Why? Because they are responsible not only for their
own holiness, but for the holiness of those they minister to.
"For they preside over men needing cure as much as over those
already cured. The vices of the crowd must be borne with in

order that they may be cured, and the plague must be endured before it is subdued. To keep here the best way of life and a mind calm and peaceful is very hard."[24]

It is always tough to lead the Christian life. And it is tougher still for the priest. St. Peter said that the devil prowls around like a roaring lion seeking to devour us.[25] We need strength, a spirit of sacrifice, and the power to resist and endure in order to overcome every obstacle and trial for the sake of the Gospel. These are the attributes of fortitude that we have been studying in these pages.

Dominican Father Louis Granada, the great spiritual master of sixteenth-century Spain, said: "We always encounter difficulties in faithfully following the path of virtue.... If fortitude is lacking, one can accomplish little in the spiritual life, even if he has the highest regard for the practice of the virtues. Such a person is as helpless as if he were bound hand and foot."[26]

If fortitude is always crucial in our spiritual lives, to my mind it is also increasingly vital in the various aspects of our priestly ministry in this cultural moment. The priest of the new evangelization is called to be a preacher and teacher of God's love in a culture of religious "privatization" and indifferentism, moral relativism, and a pervasive materialism and individualism. We are stewards of God's mysteries in a culture where people think that every mystery has been explained by science and technology. It is a culture of death, where differences between right and wrong are all broken down, and where the search for truth is often exchanged for lies, opinions, and myths.

We are missionaries in a land where people are no longer sure whether it is possible to know God; and, even if it is, they are not sure that it matters. Even among the faithful, the priest today sees the corrosive inroads that have been made by a culture that markets many competing formulas for human happiness, a culture in which the Gospel has many enemies who oppose it with deceptive teaching and strong delusion.

We need strong, courageous priests to teach, govern, and sanctify in this culture. As Father Louis of Granada said: "The Kingdom of Heaven is won only by the courageous."[27] Thus, we must cultivate the virtue of fortitude. We need men of virtue who can hold fast to sound doctrine and teaching in the face of confusion and moral laxity; to proclaim "the word of the cross," not as another ideology, philosophy, or ancient wisdom, but as "the word of power" of the living God, who was "crucified in weakness but lives by the power of God," and "being raised from the dead, will never die again."[28]

Everything in Communion with Him

According to a long-held principle of priestly formation, the priest grows in holiness through the ordinary means of his ministry.[29] Father Jordan Aumann expresses the tradition when he says, "The priest is identified with mission and… he should sanctify himself by the very works of his ministry."[30] Pope John Paul affirms this, too, at the end of his exhortation on the priesthood, *Pastores Dabo Vobis:* "The new evangelization needs new evangelizers and these are the *priests who are serious about living their priesthood as a specific path toward holiness.*"[31]

This makes sense. The priest is the man of God, especially chosen to mediate God's blessings to his people, to bring Jesus Christ into their world. It follows that there should be a unity, an integrity of life to everything the priest does. Again, I find St. Thomas's definition to be helpful — the priest should see everything in his ministry in the light of the Eucharist. He is either celebrating the Eucharist or preparing men and women for that encounter with the living God. All the mundane issues in the priest's daily work must be ordered and prioritized in this eucharistic light. Blessed Columba Marmion has said: "The great mission of the priest is to give Jesus Christ to the world."[32] This should be our question to ourselves about the things we do in our ministry — in what way do these things contribute to giving Christ to the world, to preparing our people to meet Jesus Christ in the Eucharist?

In this, as in everything he does, the priest must cultivate the intimate relationship that has been established with Christ by his ordination. Pope Benedict recommends:

> The priest needs to develop a living awareness of his ontological union with Christ, which is then expressed in his activity: *Everything I do, I do in communion with him. Precisely in doing it, I am with him.* No matter how multiple or even contradictory my activities may seem to others, they still constitute a single vocation: it is all being together with Christ, acting as an instrument in communion with him.[33]

Everything the priest does is in union with Christ. Everything contributes to his "ministry of reconciliation," of bringing all things to Christ. What this suggests is that the priest will grow in the virtues, in holiness, through the attentive, devout performance of his priestly duties. That means primarily through his daily prayer, especially the Liturgy of the Hours, through the daily celebration of the Eucharist, through his reflections on the Scriptures in preparation of his homily, through his various pastoral "rounds" and duties. The priest can also grow in virtue through all the supposedly "mundane" tasks and chores of his day, so long as he approaches them with that same "interior unity of life" in communion with Jesus Christ.

I cannot here offer more than these general remarks on priestly spiritual formation. But I must emphasize that formation in virtue has to be understood within a full program of priestly spirituality, one rooted in prayer, the Eucharist, daily reading of Scripture, daily examination of conscience, and regular confession. The advice from St. Charles Borromeo that the Church proposes in the Liturgy of the Hours remains a sound basis for the priest's daily outlook:

> Would you like me to teach you how to grow from virtue to virtue?... My brothers, you must realize that for us churchmen nothing is more necessary than meditation. We must meditate before, during, and after everything we do.... When you administer the sacraments, meditate on what you are doing. When you celebrate the Mass, reflect on the sacrifice you are offering. When you pray the office, think about the words you are saying and the Lord to whom you are speaking. When you take care of your people, meditate on the Lord's blood that has washed them clean. This is the way we can easily overcome the countless difficulties we have to face day after day, which, after all, are part of our work: in meditation we find the strength to bring Christ to birth in ourselves and in other men.[34]

Begin in Humility, Placing Absolute Confidence in God

To grow in fortitude, the priest must cultivate an attitude of humility. Humility is recognizing that our human strength is just an illusion, that God alone is the source of all strength and power. The beginning of fortitude is to know the truth that Jesus spoke to Pilate: "You would have no power... unless it had been given you from above."[35]

The spiritual master, Sulpician Father Adolphe Tanquerey, said: "The secret of our strength lies in *distrust of self* and *absolute confidence in God*."[36] It is not within our powers to make ourselves holy. We cannot come to the Father unless the Father draws us.[37] Our growth in virtue cannot be our own work, but God's work in us. As St. Thomas would have us remember: "God makes us virtuous and directs us to himself."[38]

This is easy to forget. We can mistake our zeal and our learning for moral strength and character. It is always important to fight the temptation of narcissism — that is, the temptation to perform our ministerial works for our own satisfaction rather than for the good of our people. We are apostles. We are not here for ourselves; it does not matter what we "get out of" our ministries, or how our ministries make us feel. What matters is serving the needs of our brothers and sisters — their thirst for the life-changing encounter with Jesus Christ.

To seek our own interests can distort our ministerial work. We can also be setting ourselves up to fall. Again, it is important to remember that knowledge of doctrine and even solid faith in the teachings of the Church is no guarantee of virtue. We may know what is right and true, and still be unable to do it. That was the warning of St. Paul: "I do not understand my own actions. For I do not do what I want, but I do the very thing I hate."[39] Unfortunately, this condition explains why some priests slide into sin and addiction or otherwise fail to achieve all that God would hope to accomplish through them.

The antidote to this is humility. Christian fortitude involves accepting our powerlessness apart from Christ and our total dependence upon him for our strength. It means knowing that without his grace we can do nothing and that with his grace there is nothing we cannot do. To grow in fortitude requires absolute confidence that God will provide the strength we need to serve him. He has called us to this work, he has filled us with the desire for holiness. As St. Paul said, this is his will for our lives — "our sanctification."[40] And for our holiness there is nothing he will not give us, if we do all that we can do in humility and love. The words we have often quoted from St. Paul — "I can do all things in him who strengthens me"[41] — should shape the interior life of every priest. This is the faith of the martyrs. As St. Cyprian wrote: "Christ gives strength to believers in proportion to the trust that each who receives that strength is willing to place in him."[42]

Christ will give us the strength to do what we need, but we should never fall into the trap of believing that we are in this alone. Unfortunately, this is another common temptation — for the priest to be a "loner," to think he needs no one, or worse, to think that he is spiritually superior to his colleagues in the priesthood.

Every priest is called personally, but none is called in isolation. Jesus Christ knew that we would need support and fellowship in our priestly lives. That is why he never sent his ministers out alone. He sent his disciples out two by two, in missionary pairs. The apostles exercised their priestly office in communion with their brother apostles, whom Jesus called his friends. So for us, accepting Christ's call means entering into sacred fellowship with our brother priests and bishops joined to Christ, our communion expressed in the Eucharist.

To grow in virtue, priests need these relationships of mutual support and encouragement. They need good friendships with their brother priests. They need to regard their bishop in loving obedience as a figure of Christ, and as a brother and a friend with whom they are coworkers in the apostolic service of teaching, sanctifying, and shepherding God's people. Such attitudes of filial obedience and fraternal fellowship are not always easy for men raised in a culture of excessive individualism and selfishness. So we must cultivate a spirit of humility and self-denial.

Our humility and confidence in God will be deepened by daily reflection on the Scriptures. In both the Old and New Testaments we see the truth of Christ's words: "Every one who exalts himself will be humbled, but he who humbles himself will be exalted."[43] Again and again, we find in Scripture that God confounds the strong and that, in the perceptive words of the *Catechism:* "against all human expectation God chooses those who were considered powerless and weak to show forth his faithfulness to his promises."[44]

We can also make progress through faithful prayer and meditation on the two great canticles that frame the priest's day in the Liturgy of the Hours — the "Benedictus" of Zechariah and Mary's "Magnificat."[45] During his morning prayer, the priest should bless God with Zechariah, recalling all God's acts of deliverance throughout the salvation history recounted in the Benedictus. The priest should reflect on how God — through his covenants with Abraham and David, and finally with Christ — has freed humanity from its enemies, the last enemy being death, that we might "worship him without fear."[46]

Everything we do as priests, especially our celebration of the Eucharist, is a sharing in this divine plan of salvation. We should trust in God, as Zechariah did. God has been faithful to his covenant throughout salvation history. He has made good on all his "promises of old." Thus, we can be sure he will strengthen us in our ministries.

At the end of the day, too, the priest can ask God's help, joining himself to the humble canticle of Mary. We should pray the Magnificat as ones who know that we have also been consecrated to be his servants; by our *fiat*, our "yes" to God in ordination, we know what Mary knew — that "the Almighty has done great things for me." Here again, if we pray attentively, we will hear the prayer of the Church inviting us to place our trust in God, who has been faithful to his "servant Israel" throughout salvation history. Joined to Mary, we are invited to close each day with a promise to begin fresh in his service tomorrow.

All Virtue Begins in the Sign of the Cross

Our growth in fortitude requires that we recognize ourselves as "spiritual organisms," new creations of grace in Jesus Christ.[47] The *Catechism* summarizes things directly: "The whole organism of the Christian's supernatural life has its roots in baptism."[48] In baptism, the theological and moral virtues have been infused in us and the gifts of the Spirit given to us. By this grace our natural efforts are elevated, and we are able to grow in the divine life that God has desired to place in us.

The infused virtues make us able to live as children of God and to tend toward heaven. God gives us these virtues as gifts of his love, but we must work to develop them within us. The Church proposes for our reflection in the Liturgy of the Hours these wise words from St. Columban, the great missionary abbot of the seventh century:

> It is a glorious privilege that God should grant man his eternal image and the likeness of his character.... If man applies the virtues planted in his soul to the right purpose, he will be like God. God's commands have taught us to give him back the virtues he sowed in us in our first innocence. The first command is to love our Lord with our whole heart because he loved us first, from the beginning, before our existence.[49]

The virtues have been planted in us so that we will be like God. They grow in us according to a very simple principle — namely, that practice makes perfect. We know this from experience, that the more we do something, the easier if becomes. The same is true in our moral lives. As the moral philosopher, Yves Simon, puts it: "The law of habit calls for repetitions."[50] The repetition of good behaviors done for the love of God leads to habits of moral virtue. This, in turn, will build up our

Christian character as the virtues become "second nature" in us. Progressively, we will become more like God in whose image we are created.

In seeking to grow in the virtues, we are not simply developing our own inner strengths and capacities. The growth of the spiritual organism begins and is sustained by the grace-filled initiative of God. All our moral efforts and strivings should be a grateful and loving response to his divine initiative, made possible by his grace.

As Father Romanus Cessario explains it, the infusion of the virtues means we have "a real participation in the *imitatio Christi.*" This *imitatio* is not a matter of slavishly seeking to do "what Jesus would do." Christ is far more than our role model in the moral life. He is the divine source and principle of our moral growth. Not only does he give us a set of examples and norms to live by, he gives us the "capacity to follow them."[51]

The imitation of Christ made possible by the infused virtues gives us a deep affinity with Christ. By the infusion of the virtues, we are able to join our efforts to lead a virtuous life to his own divine-human life, especially in his passion, in which we see the perfection of the virtues. "The infused virtues impress the sign of the cross onto the human virtues," Father Cessario says. The infused virtues bear the sign of Christ's death and also communicate to us the power of that death. We are joined in our weakness to the weakness of Christ's crucifixion, in order to be filled with the power of his resurrection. According to Redemptorist Father F. X. Durrwell, the spiritual theologian:

> No grace comes to us apart from the participation in Christ's death by which we rise with him into life. We must identify ourselves with Christ in his death, in his total self-renunciation, in order that we may share in the power and holiness of God.... All virtues begin with this.[52]

What this means for the priest is that all his moral efforts are aided by the promise of grace. The virtues infused in us enable us to strive with divine assistance and to know with certainty that we have been given the capacity to follow Christ's call. This is a marvelous assurance in our efforts to give ourselves completely and totally to him. We need fortitude to imitate Christ, to configure ourselves to his cross, and to grow in the sacrificial character that ordination inscribes on our beings. On a more practical level, fortitude enables us to endure the sufferings, the costs, that following Christ entails.

The Liturgy of the Hours and the Virtues

To grow in the virtue of fortitude, then, we must have an attitude of humility and a keen awareness of the divine life begun in us at baptism, in which we are "baptized into his death" and made able to "walk in newness of life."[53] According to the spiritual masters, we grow in the virtue of fortitude, as in all the virtues, through the grace we receive in the sacraments and through "meritorious acts," good works done expressly for the love of God.

Our moral life begins and ends, rises and falls, depends in everything on *prayer*. The priest should beg God daily to help him grow in the virtues, and especially in fortitude. Blessed Mother Teresa advised priests: "Pray and ask for the courage to give — 'to give until it hurts.'"[54] The priest needs to take Jesus at his word, that he will help us to grow in the virtues if we seek him in prayer: "Ask and it shall be given to you, seek and you shall find; knock and it shall be opened to you."[55]

In the New Testament, we see the example of the apostles praying that the virtues take deeper root and become the active principle of their identity and approach to the world. "Increase our faith," the Twelve implored him.[56] Paul taught us to pray for our growth in the virtues of hope[57] and love, that we might focus our lives on the excellent things, the things that truly matter.[58] So we too, as sharers in the apostolic ministry, should pray to grow in the virtues.

It would be a good pious habit for the priest and the seminarian to daily pray St. Thomas's "Prayer to Obtain the Virtues":

> Grant that I may
> through justice be subject to You,
> through prudence avoid the beguilements of the devil,
> through temperance exercise restraint,
> and through fortitude endure adversity with
> patience.[59]

In observing his daily duty of prayer, the priest will find many opportunities to petition the Lord for his strength and virtue. I cannot stress enough what a great treasure of priestly spirituality we have in the Liturgy of the Hours. As Blessed Antonio Rosmini points out, what is most significant is that in the Divine Office we pray to God in God's own words:

> Indeed, God himself places on our lips the greater part of the words in which we pray. God wrote for us in his own hand, so to speak, these most efficacious prayers, which we present to him. *This prayer embodies all man's emotions.* At times it expresses fear, then trust, sometimes compunction, again unspeakable love. It recalls to our minds so many examples — the life and death of our Lord, the faith of the patriarchs, the prophets' predictions, the apostles' preaching, the constancy of the martyrs, the heroic virtue of the confessors and virgins, etc.[60]

Father Rosmini and others have written beautiful and instructive words about the Divine Office. These should be read and reread by priests and seminarians today.[61] If we make these prayers our own, praying them with attention and devotion, then "the psalms have also a wonderful power to awaken in our hearts *the desire for every virtue*," as Pope St. Pius X said.[62] "Does the soul need light? Strength? Courage? Words wherewith to invoke God flow endlessly to our lips," Abbot Marmion reminds us.[63]

The Liturgy of the Hours, in fact, sets the priest's entire day within the contours of our humble desire for God's own strength. The first words the priest prays every day in the Office are a petition for that strength: "O God, come to my assistance; O LORD, make haste to help me."[64]

Love God and Do What You Will

This attitude of seeking God's own strength in our service of his will must animate the priest's entire day. To grow in virtue, we need to repeat virtuous acts. But we also must "supernaturalize" our motives. That means we need to make sure that everything we do, even our most menial tasks, is done for the glory of God and the fulfillment of his covenant will.

This is an ancient and still essential principle of spiritual direction in the Church. *Dilige et quod vis fac,* St. Augustine said in his famous formulation. *"Love God and do what you will."* If our actions are rooted in the motive of love, then we can only do good and only grow in virtue.[65]

In the annals of holiness in the Americas, we hear similar advice given by Father Cipriano Iñiguez Martin del Campo, who served the poor and the sick in Guadalajara, in the Mexican state of Jalisco, in the early years of the last century. Father Cipriano founded a religious order, the Servants of St. Margaret Mary and of the Poor, with the inspiring motto: "Charity, even to the point of sacrifice; and constancy even to death."

And Father Cipriano lived that motto during the anti-Catholic persecutions, when he was arrested many times and endured many hardships for the love of God. His courage and constancy was rooted in this principle — that everything we do in our priestly ministry should flow from the root of divine love. In one of his spiritual conferences, he said:

> To be a saint is to have the intention of doing all things for God. How rich and easy is the spiritual life! Why do you eat? To have the strength to serve God. Why do you sleep? Why do you obey? Not because my superior has a notebook in her hand, but to serve God.... If all that you do, you do for God, how can you do anything evil? Avoid wondering if what you are doing is the will of God, and make sure your intention is right and pure.[66]

To love God and do what we will requires a deliberate act of the will. "In order to make excellent progress in devotion, we must offer all our actions to God every day," St. Francis de Sales teaches. Literally "hundreds of times a day," we should remind ourselves that we are in God's presence and in the service of his love, the saint advises.[67]

This is great advice for the priest. By making short prayers and appeals for divine assistance and strength throughout the day we can unite ourselves more closely with Christ in all the small and ordinary actions of our days. Blessed Marmion used to advise priests that they should get into the habit of taking a moment for reflection before beginning any new task:

> To recollect oneself is to consider in the depth of one's soul the value of the act which one is about to accomplish. Learn to pray before hearing confessions, teaching catechism, or visiting the sick, and weigh the consequences of your words and actions for the eternal good of souls. Ask the Holy Spirit to enlighten your intelligence and to inflame your heart. Unite yourself with Christ; you are taking his place among men today in order to be, in his name, the instrument of grace and salvation.[68]

This principle is rooted in the apostolic teaching and the apostles' experience of Christ. St. Paul also taught: "So, whether you eat or drink, or whatever you do, do all to the glory of God.... Be imitators of me, as I am of Christ."[69] A glance at a crucifix, the touch of the rosary beads in one's pocket, a short prayer for courage — such acts of recollection can serve as an antidote to the constant barrage of the mundane and routine.

Seek Small, Daily Victories of Self-Conquest

Courage is not a virtue that is reserved only for heroic moments or emergencies. It is a virtue that will grow slowly by a thousand little acts of devotion and self-denial that we make during the course of the ordinary rounds of our days. Father Servais Pinckaers gives us wise counsel as we begin striving to grow in this virtue:

> The development of courage is progressive. It is acquired far more through small victories of self-conquest, repeated day after day, than through dreams of great actions. It grows with the dogged effort to study, to finish a task, render a service, or overcome laziness or some other fault. There will also be battles to fight, trials to encounter, small and great sufferings to endure, reaching their pitch in the illness and death of loved ones.[70]

This means that we need to approach our days in such a way that we are cooperating with the divine grace in us, practicing these little acts of devotion and dogged effort, striving every day for little victories over our selfishness. Little things matter in a big way in the spiritual life.

In general, the priest should lead a simple lifestyle, avoiding superfluous goods and attachments. While he must take care for the health of his body and mind, he should not be excessively preoccupied with his own comfort and should practice patience when he encounters the annoyances of daily life, or its ordinary discomforts, aches, and pains.[71] The more we can endure little things for the sake of Christ, the more we will find ourselves growing in the spiritual strength of the will that is fortitude.

To grow in the virtue, we also need to incorporate little acts of self-denial and detachment into our daily routines. Again, our motive must be supernatural — to grow in the love of God and to root out our tendencies to self-love. "He must increase but I must decrease." The words of the Baptist should be the priest's watchword in the spiritual life. Father Aumann reminds us:

> The goal of mortification is to strengthen oneself in the face of temptation and thereby allow virtue to develop; the purpose of self-denial is to control one's natural inclination to excessive self-love, which greedily seeks its own satisfaction, and to cultivate generous gift-love. And although difficult at the beginning, the practices of mortification can eventually become second nature, and at that point one acquires the stability and fidelity that are characteristic of fortitude.[72]

Through Many Trials We Enter the Kingdom

In this spirit of self-denial, we should bear the burdens and inconveniences of our daily ministries with a generous spirit, doing things for Christ and without complaint. The priest should never ask God to remove the crosses that come his way. Instead he should pray for the courage and the strength to carry them for and with Jesus. This attitude may be our most important key to cultivating the virtue of fortitude.

As a general matter, I believe we would all do well to return to that older form of devotion by which we were taught to "offer up" our daily struggles and hardships, all the little annoyances of our days, as a sacrificial offering for the love of God and our neighbors in the Communion of Saints. This habit would help us to increase our moral strength and deepen our capacity to suffer and persevere for the sake of the Gospel.[73]

It is also very important to recover the biblical notion of "trials" and "discipline" in the spiritual life. The hardships that come our way, the setbacks and sufferings we experience in our ministry, are never a punishment for sin or weakness. Rather, we must see them as Christ, the apostles, and the saints have all taught us to view them — as a trial or a testing from which we are to grow in holiness and the virtues.

The one certainty we have in the Christian life is that trials will come, both little and great, and it matters very much *how* we respond to them. The wisdom of the Scriptures is unwavering on this point. "Many are the afflictions of the righteous," the psalmist sings.[74] Every priest needs to take these words from Sirach to heart:

> My son, if you come forward to serve the Lord, prepare yourself for temptations. Set your heart right and be steadfast.... Cleave to him and do not depart.... Accept whatever is brought upon you, and in changes that humble you, be patient. For gold is tested in fire, and acceptable men made in the furnace of humiliation. Trust in him and he will help you.[75]

Jesus told his apostles to anticipate persecution and tribulation.[76] Throughout the New Testament, we see the apostles reminding themselves of this teaching. Exhorting the disciples, Paul told them that it is "through many trials we must enter the Kingdom of God."[77] Again, matter of factly, he writes to the pastor Timothy: "Indeed, all who desire to live a godly life in Christ Jesus will be persecuted."[78]

The letter to the Hebrews tells us to consider our sufferings to be the "discipline" of our loving Father. Through this discipline we are strengthened to grow up into the image of his Son, who himself endured hostility from sinners and was chastised for our sake. The Father "disciplines us for our good, that we may share his holiness... the peaceful fruit of righteousness to those who have been trained by it."[79]

St. Thomas Aquinas also taught that God sends us afflictions in order "to encourage virtue."[80] Interpreting an image in the Gospel of John, Thomas says that God "prunes" us through hardships.

> Thus the Vinedresser prunes away the extra shoots so that the vine can bear more fruit. It is the same with us. For if we are well-disposed and united to God, yet scatter our love over many things, our virtue becomes weak and we become less able to do good. This is why God, in order that we may bear fruit, will frequently remove such obstacles and *prune us by sending troubles and temptations, which make us stronger....* And he does this so that it may bear more fruit, that is, *grow in virtue.*[81]

Thomas here reflects the consistent teaching of the Scriptures. Paul, too, envisions a kind of pattern of spiritual growth that comes through our acceptance of our trials in faith. What he is describing is growth in the virtue of fortitude, which becomes the core of a mature Christian character and spirituality. God in his grace comes to our assistance so that by our patient endurance our character grows through hope in Christ's resurrection and the certainty of our own:

> We rejoice in our hope of sharing the glory of God. More than that, we rejoice in our sufferings knowing that suffering produces endurance, and endurance produces

character and character produces hope, and hope does not disappoint us.[82]

Imitation of the Mysteries of Christ

We are called to patient endurance by Jesus Christ, who suffered for us, leaving us an example that we should "follow in his steps."[83] We have considered how the *imitatio Christi* is at the heart of priestly spirituality. And as Father Tanquerey has written, this *imitatio* is the principle for growth in the spiritual life:

> At the bottom the Gospel is no more than a relation to the deeds and traits of our Lord's sacred person proposed to us as a model for our imitation: "All that Jesus began *to do and to teach*" (Acts 1:1). Christianity in turn is nothing more than the imitation of Christ. St. Paul gave this as the sum total of our duties: "Be you followers of me as I also am of Christ" (1 Cor. 4:16; 11:1; Eph. 5:1).[84]

To imitate Christ in his virtues means we have to develop a deep interior friendship with him. The relationship we are called to is a true, lifelong friendship that grows daily through our prayerful contemplation of the mysteries of Christ's life as they are presented to us in the Gospel.

The priest must learn to read the Scriptures in a spirit of *lectio divina*, in a prayerful and intimate dialogue, seeking the face of Christ who comes to speak to us in the sacred pages. We need to read, not as students, but as friends or lovers. We need to read as ones seeking a deeper fellowship with our beloved; as ones who want to share in our friend's thoughts and feelings, and participate in his very life. The holy priest St. Josemaría Escrivá de Balaguer the founder of Opus Dei, explains very well the ways and means of this contemplative reading.

To be Christ himself, we must *see ourselves in him*. It is not enough to have a general idea of the spirit of Jesus' life; we have to learn the details of his life and, through them, his attitudes. And especially, we must contemplate his life to derive from it strength, light, serenity, peace. When you love someone, you want to know all about his life and character so as to become like him. That is why we have to meditate on the life of Jesus, from his birth in a stable right up to his death and resurrection....

In this way we become involved in his life. It is not a matter of just thinking about Jesus, of recalling some scenes of his life. We must be completely involved and play a part in his life. We should follow him as closely as Mary his mother did, as closely as the first Twelve, the holy women, the crowds that pressed about him. If we do this without holding back, Christ's words will enter deep into our soul and will really change us. For "the Word of God is living and active, sharper than any two-edged sword, piercing to the division of the soul and spirit, of joints and marrow, and discerning the thoughts and intentions of the heart" (Heb. 4:12).[85]

Daily reading of the Scriptures, especially the Gospels, is essential for our growth in our priestly identity and in the virtues of Christ. But we need to remember, as St. Josemaría tells us, that we are not reading human words but the very Word of God. We are not reading for "information" or even for knowledge. We are reading to meet the living God and to be transformed gradually, day by day, in that encounter.

The Word of God is the only word that has the power to truly transform us. God spoke and through his Word the heavens and the earth were created. Through his Word, men and women were healed and even raised from the dead. And through his Word, spoken by his ministers at the altar, the bread and wine are made his Body and Blood. We must read Scripture "not as the word of men, but as what it really is, the Word of God, which is at work in you who believe."[86]

Daily devotion to the Rosary, in which we meditate on the mysteries of Christ's life as seen through the eyes of Mary, will be a great aid to the priest. In the normal rhythms of his daily ministry, the priest will also find a rich opportunity to allow the divine Word to "work" in him. Each day the priest says Mass, and in each Mass a passage from the Gospel is read. The priest should get in the daily habit of spending a little time prayerfully reading that day's Gospel selection. The priest will find many practical lessons and examples of Jesus' own strength of soul and fortitude. More than that, he will find himself gradually growing in the image of Christ.

As the saints know, there is a purpose and a spiritual power in the Church's liturgical cycle of readings, especially in the Gospels. During the course of the Church's liturgical year, we are presented day by day with the life of Christ — his incarnation, birth, and "hidden life"; his public teaching and ministry; his passion and death; his resurrection, ascension, and sending of the Holy Spirit.

Following Jesus, contemplating these mysteries, our love for him grows, and we gradually come to a deeper understanding of the heart and the mind of Christ. Through our daily encounter we are being refashioned in the *imago Christi*, through the power of God's Word working in us. As Blessed Marmion says:

> Each year, as the soul follows the liturgical cycle, it shares ever more intimately in these mysteries, and is identified more and more with Christ, with his thoughts, his feelings, his life.... Gradually it is transformed into the likeness of the divine model — not only because this model is represented in each stage of his terrestrial existence,

but above all because a divine virtue goes out from these mysteries to sanctify us, according to the measure of our faith.[87]

From Virtue to Virtue: The Spirituality of Martyrdom

In the end, the priest's program of growth in virtue and holiness has already been given to him in the words of his bishop at ordination: "Know what you are doing and imitate the mystery you celebrate."[88] These words set our ministries and our lives in the context of the eucharistic mystery, the mystery of our Lord's laying down his life, offering his Body and Blood for the life of the world.

We have been chosen to share in this mystery of his life, death, resurrection, and ascension. The priest can say with St. Paul: "For his sake I have suffered the loss of all things... that I may know him and the power of his resurrection... becoming like him."[89] We have been chosen to know him, to follow him, and to be like him — not as students of a school of thought or as servants of a master, but as *friends*. "I have called you friends," he says to us.[90] And he has opened his own life to us, making it possible for us to reflect his glory in our own lives. This is the joy of the priesthood.

Thomas Aquinas, as we have discussed, believed the martyrs offer the most perfect example of fortitude and the most perfect imitation of Christ. The martyrs withhold nothing, offering even their own lives in their love of God. And as we have seen, the martyrs experienced the deep friendship of Christ standing alongside them, strengthening them in their sufferings. In their weakness, the power of Christ was upon them.[91]

The spirituality of the martyrs is rooted in the virtue of fortitude, which gives them the power to endure want and suffering, toil, pain, and hardships — to overcome their natural fear of death — all for the love of God. That is why the cultivation of this virtue is so essential in our priesthood. Because the spirituality of the martyrs is the essential spirituality of our *amoris officium*, the office of love that is the priesthood.

"The ideal of martyrdom exists at the heart of all Christian spirituality, of every life intent on the practice of the Gospel," Father Pinckaers says. "It is the spirituality of the following of Christ in love."[92]

Love, as Jesus taught, is the willingness to lay down one's life for another in the love of God. Thus the spirituality of the martyrs moves us toward the central mystery of our faith, and the central mystery of our priestly life, the Eucharist. As we have observed, the earliest martyrs understood their deaths in liturgical or eucharistic terms. As Christ offered his body and blood on the cross, and again in the Eucharist, the martyrs knew themselves to be offering their bodies and blood in sacrifice. "Just as he had partaken of a gift of self at the table of the Lord, so he prepared to offer such a gift," St. Augustine said of the martyrdom of the deacon, St. Lawrence.[93]

The first Christian priests, the apostles, understood their ministries and lives in these same eucharistic terms. We are "a holy priesthood to offer spiritual sacrifices acceptable to God," St. Peter writes.[94] Paul went so far as to talk about his own life being a kind of liturgy — a libation, a sacrificial offering made in faith.[95] Again and again we hear that the most perfect sacrifice, the sacrifice most desired and pleasing to God, is the offering of our own lives in the service of God's covenant will.[96]

"Present your bodies as a living sacrifice, holy and acceptable to God, which is your spiritual worship," Paul wrote. We are meant to become a "sacrifice of praise."[97] This is the spirituality that the priest must bring to the altar each day in the Mass, as we are called to participate in Jesus' own offering of his life to God in love.

The cross of Christ should give the basic shape to our priestly spirituality. What I mean is that our life should be a dying to self and a living for Christ and his Gospel. The holy Pope St. Gregory the Great once said: "It is not so difficult for a man to give up the things that belong to him, but it is very difficult to give up himself."[98] This is true. Yet this is the imitation of Christ in his passion to which we are called. As St. Thomas said:

> For since he dies for us, we, too, should die to ourselves, that is, deny ourselves for him: "If any man would come after me, let him deny himself and take up his cross daily and follow me" (Luke 9:23). This is the same as saying: let him die to himself. But because Christ rose for us, we should so die to sin and to the old life and to ourselves that we might rise to the new life of Christ.... This is why the Lord not only said, "Let him deny himself and take up his cross," but he added, "and follow me" — namely, in newness of life, by advancing in the virtues: "They shall go from virtue to virtue" (Ps. 84:7).[99]

The old Vulgate translation of Psalm 84:7 gives us a vivid image of the progress we seek in our spiritual lives. We want to grow *from virtue to virtue*. In all our efforts we are entrusted to the patronage of Mary, the Mother of Christ and the mother of priests. Mary is the strong and holy woman foretold in the Scriptures. In her courage, she accepted the gift of the Holy Spirit, conceived, and gave birth to the Virtue of God.[100] As she stood at the foot of the cross, Christ entrusted his first priests, the apostles, to her motherly care.

It must be said: every priest needs a strong devotion to the Blessed Mother. Many of us are aware in a deep way that we owe our vocations to the prayers and sacrifices of our earthly mothers. Our heavenly Mother, with all the love of her maternal heart, continues to pray for us in our efforts to serve in the person of her son. It was Christ's dying wish that his priests behold her as their mother. My prayer at the end of this book is that we too will behold Mary as our mother, and seek her help in growing in the virtue and gift of fortitude given to us by our gracious God.

May we grow through our imitation of the mysteries of her Son and our service of his Gospel, no matter what opposition or resistance we might face, no matter what our trials and difficulties. And may it be said of every priest of the new evangelization: *His heart was courageous in the ways of the LORD.*[101]

Endnotes

Chapter 1: The Beginning of Strong Courage

1. Ubaldus da Rieti, O.F.M., *Life of Venerable Fr. Antony Margil* (New York City: Franciscan Missionary Printing Press, 1910), 10.

2. John Tracy Ellis, ed., *Documents of American Catholic History*, 2 vols. (Chicago: Henry Regnery, 1967), 1:25.

3. *Catechism of the Catholic Church*, 2d. ed. (Vatican City: Libreria Editrice, 1997), no. 828.

4. Compare Rom. 1:7; 1 Cor. 1:2.

5. Phil. 4:8.

6. Wis. 8:7.

7. *About the Ends of Goods and Evils*, bk. 5, chap. 23, 67; compare *On Duties of the Clergy*, bk. 1, chap. 2, 5.

8. *On the Duties of the Clergy*, bk. 1, chap. 24, 115. Compare Jordan Aumann, *Spiritual Theology* (Huntington, IN: Our Sunday Visitor, 1980), 87.

9. Compare Matt. 7:13.

10. *A Brief Reader on the Virtues of the Human Heart* (San Francisco: Ignatius, 1991), 9.

11. "On the Rehabilitation of Virtue," republished in *American Catholic Philosophical Quarterly* 79:1 (2005): 21–37, at 22.

12. *Of the Christian Faith*, bk. 3, chap. 7, 49, 52–53.

13. *Commentary on the Song of Songs*, bk. 1.

14. Compare Rom. 5:14; 8:29; 1 Cor. 15:45, 49; Col. 1:15; 3:10; Gen. 1:27.

15. *Catechism*, no. 1811.

16. Rom. 5:5.

17. Rom. 8:14–16; 1 Cor. 13:13; compare *Catechism*, no. 1813.

18. See also Acts 3:15; Wis. 8:7; 2 Pet. 1:5–7, 11; 2 Cor. 9:10; Gal. 3:5; *Catechism*, nos. 1266, 1833. See also, Aumann, *Spiritual Theology*, 86.

19. Compare Eph. 4:15; Phil. 1:9; Rom. 15:13; 2 Pet. 3:18.

20. Quoted in St. Thomas Aquinas, *Summa Theologiae*, pt. 1a–2ae, q. 55, art. 4. See also Romanus Cessario, *The Virtues, or the Examined Life* (New York: Continuum, 2002), 100–105.

21. *Catechism*, no. 1828; Cessario, *The Virtues, or the Examined Life*, 11.

22. Compare Isa. 11:1–3; *Catechism*, nos. 1830–1831.

23. Gregory, *Oration and Panegyric Addressed to Origen*, 12.

24. *The Beatitudes*, Sermon 1. See also *Catechism*, no. 1803.

25. 2 Cor. 3:18.

26. Augustine, *Commentary on the Psalms*, 94, 15; compare John G. Arintero, O.P., *The Mystical Evolution in the Development and Vitality of the Church*, 2 vols. (Rockford, IL: TAN, 1978), 1:205–206.

27. Compare Matt. 5:48; Lev. 19:2.

28. 1 Thess. 4:3.

29. *Catechism*, nos. 2013–2014.

30. *Spiritual Theology*, 247.

31. Compare John 13:34.

32. *Catechism*, no. 1813.

33. *Catechism*, no. 1844; compare nos. 1827, 1840, 1968.

34. *Of the Morals of the Catholic Church*, chap. 15, 25; compare Servais Pinckaers, O.P., *Sources of Christian Ethics* (Washington, DC: Catholic University, 2005), 27; Arintero, *The Mystical Evolution*, 1:208.

35. Compare *Catechism*, no. 1974.

36. *Oeuvres*, 5:251; quoted in Canon F. Cuttaz, *Our Life of Grace* (Notre Dame, IN: Fides, 1958), 183.

37. See Eph. 5:1; 1 John 4:8.

38. *Summa*, pt. 1a–2ae, q. 61, art. 4.

39. See, especially, Alasdair MacIntyre, *After Virtue: A Study in Moral Theory*, 2nd. ed. (Notre Dame, IN: University of Notre Dame, 1984).

40. See Pope John Paul II, *Fides et Ratio*, Encyclical Letter on the Relationship between Faith and Reason (September 14, 1998), 98.

41. Pinckaers, *Sources of Christian Ethics*, 375.

42. Joseph Cardinal Ratzinger, "The Renewal of Moral Theology: Perspectives of Vatican II and *Veritatis Splendor*," *Communio* 32 (Summer 2005): 357–368, at 358–359. See also Pinckaers, "Moral Theology in the Modern Era of the Manuals," in *Sources of Christian Ethics*, 254–279.

43. Quoted in Pope Pius XI, *Ad Catholici Sacerdotii*, Encyclical Letter on the Catholic Priesthood (December 20, 1935), 34. Compare Antonio Rosmini, *Talks to Priests* (New York: New City, 1982), 15.

44. *Summa*, suppl., q. 35, art. 1, reply obj. 3; compare pt. 2a–2ae, q. 184, art. 8; see also Pius XI, *Ad Catholici Sacerdotii*, 35.

45. Matt. 9:13; Rom. 3:10.

46. 1 Cor. 11:4.

47. *Ad Catholici Sacerdotii*, 36.

48. Code of Canon Law, no. 276.

49. Office of Readings (October 19), *The Liturgy of the Hours According to the Roman Rite*, 4 vols. (New York: Catholic Book Publishing, 1975), 4:1505–1506.

50. See such standard works as Adolphe Tanquerey, S.S., *The Spiritual Life: A Treatise on Ascetical and Mystical Theology*, 2nd. rev. ed. (Rockford, IL: TAN, 2000 [1930]), 472–589; Arintero, *The Mystical Evolution*, 1:204–215; R. Garrigou–Lagrange, O.P., *The Three Ages of the Interior Life: Prelude to Eternal Life*, 2 vols. (Rockford, IL: TAN, 1989 [1947]), 1:52–65; Cuttaz,

Our Life of Grace, 171–183; Matthias J. Scheeben, *The Glories of Divine Grace* (Rockford, IL: TAN, 2000 [1946]), 183–217.

51. Second Vatican Council, *Prebyterorum Ordinis*, Decree on the Ministry and Life of Priests (December 7, 1965), 12–13; *Optatum Totius*, Decree on Priestly Training (October 8, 1965), 8.

52. *Pastores Dabo Vobis*, Post-Synodal Apostolic Exhortation on the Formation of Priests in the Circumstances of the Present Day (March 25, 1992), 26–28. For other mentions of the importance of the virtues in priestly formation in recent magisterial documents, see *Code of Canon Law* (Washington, DC: Canon Law Society of America, 1999), no. 245; *Presbyterorum Ordinis*, 3; Congregation for the Clergy, *Directory on the Ministry and Life of Priests* (Vatican City: Libreria Editrice, 1994), 75.

53. *Program of Priestly Formation* (Washington, DC: United States Conference of Catholic Bishops, 2006), 76. Compare 110, 260, 267.

54. Congregation for Catholic Education, *Guidelines for the Use of Psychology in the Admission and Formation of Candidates for the Priesthood* (June 28, 2008), 3, compare 2, 5, 9, 14.

55. Celebration of Vespers and Meeting with the Bishops of the United States of America (April 16, 2008).

56. *Ecclesia in America*, Post-Synodal Apostolic Exhortation on the Encounter with the Living Jesus Christ: The Way to Conversion, Communion and Solidarity in America (January 22, 1999), 6.

57. *Presbyterorum Ordinis*, 10; *Optatum Totius*, 20.

58. Pope John Paul II, *Redemptoris Missio*, Encyclical Letter on the Permanent Validity of the Church's Missionary Mandate (December 7, 1990), 67.

59. *Presbyterorum Ordinis*, 14.

60. Lynn Bridgers, *Death's Deceiver: The Life of Joseph P. Machebeuf* (Albuquerque: University of New Mexico, 1997), 205.

61. Bridgers, *Death's Deceiver*, 210.

62. *Archbishop Lamy: In His Own Words*, ed. and trans. Father Thomas J. Steele, S.J. (Albuquerque, NM: LPD Press, 2000), 213, 215.

63. *Archbishop Lamy: In His Own Words*, 116–117.

64. See *Summa*, pt. 2a–2ae, q. 137, a. 2.

65. *The Four Cardinal Virtues* (Notre Dame, IN: University of Notre Dame, 1976), 3.

66. Ambrose, *Duties of the Clergy*, bk. 1, chap. 35, 39. Compare *Summa*, pt. 2a–2ae, q. 123, art. 2.

67. Pope John Paul II, Address to the Clergy and Male Religious of Palermo (November 20, 1982); text in *Origins* (December 6, 1982): 12. Quoted in David L. Toups, *Reclaiming Our Priestly Character* (Omaha, NE: Institute for Priestly Formation, 2008), 134.

68. Cessario, *The Virtues, or the Examined Life*, 99–100; Ratzinger, "The Church's Teaching: Authority–Faith–Morals," in Heinz Schürmann,

Joseph Cardinal Ratzinger, and Hans Urs von Balthasar, *Principles of Christian Morality* (San Francisco: Ignatius, 1986), 62–63.

69. 1 Cor. 2:16.

70. *The Sources of Christian Ethics,* 20. Emphasis added.

71. *The Virtues, or the Examined Life,* 12.

72. Heb. 11:33–34.

73. John 16:33.

74. *The Virtues, or the Examined Life,* 167.

75. *Of the Christian Faith,* bk. 3, chap. 7, 53. Emphasis added.

76. *Nothingness Itself: Selected Writings of Ven. Fr. Antonio Margil, 1690–1724,* trans. Benedict Leutenegger, O.F.M., ed. Marion A. Habig, O.F.M. (Chicago: Franciscan Herald, 1976), 322.

Chapter 2: All Things in Him Who Strengthens Me

1. Ciszek and Daniel L. Flaherty, *He Leadeth Me* (San Francisco: Ignatius, 1995), 67, 68, 70; on his early years, see Cizek and Flaherty, *With God in Russia* (New York: Image, 1966).

2. See also John 13:20; 17:18.

3. *Pastores Dabo Vobis,* 5.

4. St. John Chrysostom, *On the Priesthood,* bk. 3, chap. 5.

5. See Heb. 5:1–3.

6. *Presbytorum Ordinis,* 3; *Directory on the Ministry and Life of Priests,* 75.

7. Mark 1:15; Luke 11:28.

8. *Pastores Dabo Vobis,* 43.

9. On the confusion of priestly identity in the years after Vatican II, see Toups, *Reclaiming Our Priestly Character,* 99–105.

10. 2 Tim. 1:9.

11. John 15:5.

12. John 5:19, 30.

13. "The Nature of the Priesthood," Address to the Opening of the Eighth Ordinary Assembly of the Synod of Bishops on Priestly Formation (October 1, 1990), in *The Essential Pope Benedict XVI: His Central Writings and Speeches,* eds. John F. Thorton and Susan B. Varenne (San Francisco: HarperSanFrancisco, 2007), 297. Emphasis added.

14. See Heb. 3:1; compare Acts 3:13; Rom. 15:8; James 1:1; 1 Thess. 3:2; Titus 1:1.

15. John 15:15.

16. John 20:21.

17. 2 Cor. 12:5, 9–10.

18. Eph. 3:16; Rom. 8:26.

19. See generally, Myles McDonnell, *Roman Manliness:* Virtus *and the Roman Republic* (Cambridge: Cambridge University, 2007).

20. *Apology,* 42.

21. *Discourses on the First Decade of Titus Livius,* bk. 2, chap. 2.

22. A. Gauthier, "Fortitude," in A. M. Henry, ed. *The Virtues and States of Life* (Chicago: Fides, 1957), 491.

23. See Rahner's essay, "Men in the Church," in *Mission and Grace: Essays in Pastoral Theology*, vol. 2 (New York: Sheed and Ward, 1964), 68–104.

24. *Is Celibacy Outdated?* (Newman Press, 1965), 64–66.

25. Address to Clergy at Warsaw Cathedral (May 25, 2006); compare Toups, *Reclaiming Our Priestly Character*, 147–148.

26. For instance, in the replacement of Judas in the apostolic college (Acts 1:21), and in the ordination of seven "men" (*andres*) in Acts 6:3.

27. Congregation for the Doctrine of the Faith, *Inter Insigniores*, Declaration Regarding the Question of the Admission of Women to Ministerial Priesthood (October 15, 1976), 5.

28. *Inter Insigniores*, 5. The implications of these insights for an authentic understanding of masculinity and femininity, especially as they relate to ordained and nonordained ministry in the Church, have yet to be fully developed by theologians and other pastoral agents. I hope that faithful theologians, psychologists, and others will find this to be a fertile area for future research.

29. *Pastores Dabo Vobis*, 73.

30. *Life of Coriolanus*, 1.

31. *Tusculan Disputations*, 2:18.

32. See Christian Cochini, S.J., *The Apostolic Origins of Priestly Celibacy* (San Francisco: Ignatius, 1990).

33. See James P. Socias, comp., *Priesthood in the Third Millennium: Addresses of Pope John Paul II 1993* (Chicago: Midwest Theological Forum, 1994), 81–86, 143–149; Thomas Acklin, O.S.B., *The Unchanging Heart of the Priesthood* (Steubenville, OH: Emmaus Road, 2005), 101–124.

34. Pope John Paul II, *Memory and Identity: Conversations at the Dawn of a Millennium* (New York: Rizzoli, 2005), 28–29.

35. 1 Tim. 5:2. On priests' relationships with women, see Pope John Paul II, *Letter to Priests for Holy Thursday* (1995), esp. at 5.

36. *With God in Russia*, 104.

37. John 6:38.

38. 2 Cor. 6:4; 5:20.

39. 2 Cor. 12:9.

40. Phil. 4:13.

41. *He Leadeth Me*, 70.

Chapter 3: Contempt of Death and the Crown of Life

1. *Church History*, bk. 8, chap. 12, 7.

2. *Letter* 39. The story of Celerinus is also told in Ludwig Hertling and Englebert Kirschbaum, *The Roman Catacombs and Their Martyrs* (Milwaukee: Bruce, 1956), 111–112.

3. *To the Romans*, 5–6.

4. *The Martyrdom of Polycarp*, in *Readings in Church History*, ed. Colman J. Barry (Westminster, MD: Christian Classics, 1985), 70–74, at 73.

5. *Oration in Praise of Constantine*, chap. 7, 7.

6. See the discussion in Rodney Stark, *The Rise of Christianity* (San Francisco: HarperSanFrancisco, 1997), 83.

7. Quoted in Eusebius, *The History of the Church*, bk. 7, chap. 22.

8. Cyprian, *On the Mortality*, 15. See also Stark, *The Rise of Christianity*, 81.

9. *Second Apology*, chap. 12.

10. *The Four Cardinal Virtues*, 117.

11. *Discourses*, bk. 4, chap. 7. See also Robert L. Wilken, *The Christians as the Romans Saw Them* (New Haven: Yale University, 1984), 82.

12. *Meditations*, bk. 11, 3. See also Wilken, *The Christians as the Romans Saw Them*, 82.

13. Quoted in Wilken, *The Christians as the Romans Saw Them*, 80. See also David Batson, *The Treasure Chest of the Early Christians: Faith, Care, and Community from the Apostolic Age to Constantine the Great* (Grand Rapids, MI: Eerdmans, 2001), 90–91.

14. On the contrast between Christian morals and that of the Empire at large, see Stark, *The Rise of Christianity*, 104, 115–128.

15. For Paul's assimilation of the virtues, see Pinckaers, *Sources of Christian Morality*, 125–134.

16. Second Vatican Council, *Gaudium et Spes*, Pastoral Constitution on the Church in the Modern World (December 7, 1965), 22.

17. *Christians Among the Virtues: Theological Conversations with Ancient and Modern Ethics* (Notre Dame, 1997), 68.

18. Aquinas, *Super Boethium de Trinitate* [Commentary on Boethius's On the Trinity], q. 2, art. 3.

19. See Stanley Hauerwaus, "The Difference of Virtue and the Difference it Makes: Courage Exemplified," *Modern Theology* 9:3 (July 1993): 249–264.

20. *Nicomachean Ethics*, bk. 3 7, 1115a10–35.

21. *Nicomachean Ethics*, bk. 3, 6.

22. *Nicomachean Ethics*, bk. 3, 6.

23. *Nicomachean Ethics*, bk. 3, 6, 1115a 28–1115b5.

24. "The Virtue of Courage in Mencius," in *Courage*, ed. Barbara Darling-Smith, Boston University Studies in Philosophy and Religion 23 (Notre Dame, IN: University of Notre Dame, 2002), 65–79, at 79, n. 4. Emphasis added.

25. Mary Louise Carlson, "Pagan Examples of Fortitude in the Latin Christian Apologists," *Classical Philology* 43:2 (April 1948), 93–104, at 95.

26. *Ab Urbe Condita*, 2, 13.

27. For other examples, see Carlson, "Pagan Examples of Fortitude," 95.

28. *Roman Manliness*, 25.

29. *Laches* 191D-E, in *Laches and Charmides,* trans. Rosamond Kent Sprague (Indianapolis: Hackett, 1973), 33. See also the discussion of courage in Plato's *Republic* 429Cff and *Laws* 633C–D.

30. *Tusculan Disputations,* bk. 3, 17, 36.

31. *Tusculan Disputations,* bk. 4, 14, 41–42; compare bk. 2, 18, 43, where Cicero writes that "there are two main functions [of fortitude], namely scorn of death and scorn of pain." See also Cicero's *De inventione,* bk. 2, 163 (Fortitude is "undertaking dangers and enduring toils after full reflection."). Compare Aquinas, *Summa,* pt. 2a–2ae, q. 123, art. 3.

32. *De officiis,* bk. 3, 33, 117.

33. Acts 18:12–17.

34. *Epistle* 67, 6.

35. *Christians among the Virtues,* 114.

36. "Fortitude," 497–498.

37. *Life of Pericles,* 1–4; quoted in Wilken's fine chapter on "Likeness to God," in his *The Spirit of Early Christian Thought,* 262–290.

38. 1 John 3:2.

39. *On the Duties of the Clergy,* bk. 1, chap. 36, 179, 181.

40. Ambrose treats fortitude in *On the Duties of the Clergy,* bk. 1, chaps. 35–42, 175–218.

41. *On the Duties of the Clergy,* bk. 1, chap. 36, 183.

42. *On the Duties of the Clergy,* bk. 1, chap. 37, 186.

43. *On the Duties of the Clergy,* bk. 1, chap. 36, 182.

44. *On the Duties of the Clergy,* bk. 1, chap. 37, 186.

45. "Pagan Examples of Fortitude," 96.

46. "Pagan Examples of Fortitude," 102.

47. *The Epitome of the Divine Institutes,* chap. 39.

48. *The Divine Institutes,* chap. 14.

49. *On the Martyrs,* chap. 4.

50. *The City of God,* bk. 1, chap. 15.

51. *The City of God,* bk. 1, chap. 24.

52. Gregory, *Morals on the Book of Job,* bk. 7, chap. 21; quoted in *Summa,* pt. 2a–2ae, q. 123, art. 3, obj. 1.

53. *On Christian Doctrine,* bk. 2, chap. 7; quoted in *Summa,* pt. 2a–2ae, q. 139, art. 1, obj. 3.

54. *Commentary on the Gospel according to St. Luke,* bk. 5, 42.

55. Gregory, *Morals on the Book of Job,* bk. 7, chap. 21; quoted in *Summa,* 2a-2ae, 123, art. 4, reply obj. 1.

56. *Of the Morals of the Catholic Church,* bk. 1, chap. 15; quoted in *Summa,* pt. 2a–2ae, q. 123, art. 4.

57. Wilken, *The Spirit of Early Christian Thought,* 265.

58. *Martyrs of Palestine,* chap. 2.

59. *Decretum Gelasianum,* 4.4; translation adapted from http://www.tertullian.org/decretum_eng.htm. Latin text at: http://www.thelatinlibrary.

com/decretum.html. Also quoted in Rodney Stark, *The Rise of Christianity* (San Francisco: HarperSanFranciso, 1997), 182.

60. Heb. 2:15.

61. Compare 1 Cor. 1:18.

62. Compare 1 Cor. 15:26.

63. *To the Nations*, bk. 1, chap. 19.

64. See Robin Darling Young, *In Procession before the World: Martyrdom as Public Liturgy in Early Christianity* (Milwaukee: Marquette University, 2001); Mike Aquilina, *The Resilient Church: The Glory, the Shame, and the Hope for Tomorrow* (Ijamsville, MD: Word Among Us, 2007), 18–19.

65. Joseph Cardinal Ratzinger, *Pilgrim Fellowship of Faith: The Church as Communion* (San Francisco: Ignatius, 2005), 112–113.

66. *The Martyrdom of Polycarp*, 9. *Acts of the Christian Martyrs*, 8–9.

67. Compare Rom. 12:1.

68. *The Martyrdom of Pionius the Presbyter and His Companions*, 19, in *The Acts of the Christian Martyrs*, introd., trans. Herbert Musurillo (Oxford: Clarendon, 1972), 160–161.

69. *Martyrdom of Pionius*, 21; in *Acts of the Christian Martyrs*, 162–163.

Chapter 4: The Lord Is My Strength

1. See "Father Emil Kapaun, 1916–1951," in Ann Ball, *Faces of Holiness: Modern Saints in Photos and Words* (Huntington, IN: Our Sunday Visitor, 1998), 87–96, quote at 88.

2. Ball, "Father Emil Kapaun," 91.

3. Ball, "Father Emil Kapaun," 95.

4. "Fortitude," 499.

5. Jer. 9:23–24; see also Ps. 32:16–17.

6. *The Institutes*, bk. 11, 11.

7. See 1 Cor. 4:7; James 1:17.

8. *Talks to Priests*, 153.

9. Isa. 10:12–13; see also Isa. 22:17.

10. Ezek. 28:1.

11. Ezek. 28:13, 14, 16.

12. Ezek. 28:4–5.

13. Deut. 8:17–18. Emphasis added.

14. *Catechism*, no. 1541.

15. *Catechism*, nos. 401, 309.

16. Compare Gen. 12, 22; John 11:52; 2 Cor. 6:16.

17. Exod. 19:6.

18. See Gal. 6:16.

19. 1 Pet. 2:9; Rev. 1:6; 5:10.

20. Compare Num. 1:48-53; Josh. 13:33; *Catechism*, no. 1539.

21. Jean Colson, *Ministre de Jésus-Christ ou le Sacerdoce de l'Evangile* (Paris: Beachesne, 1966), 185; quoted in Joseph Cardinal Ratzinger, *Called*

to Communion: Understanding the Church Today* (San Francisco: Ignatius, 1996), 127.

22. See Deut. 10:9.

23. Ps. 16:5.

24. Pope Benedict XVI, Address to the Members of the Roman Curia at the Traditional Exchange of Christmas Greetings (December 22, 2006).

25. *Catechism,* no. 1554; compare 1 Tim. 2:5. See generally, Albert Vanhoye, *Old Testament Priests and the New Priest* (Petersham, MA: St. Bede's, 1986).

26. Compare Mark 3:14 (Greek: *epoiēsen*); 1 Kings 12:31; 13:33; see also Pope Benedict XVI, *Jesus of Nazareth* (New York: Doubleday, 2007), 171.

27. *Catechism,* no. 611.

28. See Gen. 12:2; 22:18; Gal. 3:8–9, 27–29.

29. *Catechism,* nos. 1079, 1082.

30. See Deut. 4:37; 7:12.

31. Ps. 64:7.

32. Exod. 13:3, 14; 4:34; Ps. 89:10.

33. Pss. 50:1; 132:2, 5; Isa. 24:1; 49:26; 60:16.

34. 1 Chron. 16:11; Ps. 105:4.

35. Isa. 40:29, 31.

36. Ps. 27:13–14.

37. Ps. 30:24.

38. Ps. 18:2, 31–32; see also Jer. 16:19; Hab. 3:19.

39. Exod. 15:2.

40. Exod. 2:24; compare Ezek. 16:60–61; Jer. 14:21; Ps. 106:45; Exod. 6:5.

41. Ps. 68:35; see also Pss. 17:32, 39; 28:7–8; 46:1.

42. Deut. 31:1–3.

43. Deut. 31:6, 7, 23.

44. Josh. 1:9; see also Josh. 1:6, 7, 18; 10:25.

45. 1 Chron. 28:20.

46. James 5:10–11.

47. James 5:10–11; See J. R. Baskin, "Job as Moral Exemplar in Ambrose," *Vigiliae Christianae* 35 (1981): 222–231; at 222.

48. *Morals on the Book of Job,* pref., quoted in Jean Daniélou, S.J., *Holy Pagans of the Old Testament* (London: Longman, Green, 1957), 98.

49. Daniélou, *Holy Pagans,* 97.

50. Mic. 6:6–8.

51. Ps. 40:6–8.

52. Matt. 9:13; 12:7.

53. Rom. 12:1; Eph. 1:6; Heb. 13:15.

54. Ps. 50:14–15, 23.

55. Some commonly recognized *tōdāh* psalms are Pss. 18; 30; 32; 41; 66; 116; 118; 138. See the classification in Hermann Gunkel, *An Introduction to the Psalms* (Macon, GA: Mercer University, 1988), 199–221.

56. Ps. 18:20–27.

57. Ps. 18:17, 48.

58. Ps. 18:4–5.

59. Ps. 18:6.

60. Ps. 18:16–19.

61. Ps. 18:32, 39.

62. Ps. 18:28–29.

63. "The Origins of the Lord's Supper," in *Essays on Biblical Theology* (Minneapolis: Augsburg, 1981), 117–140, at 132.

64. Joseph Cardinal Ratzinger, "Form and Content in the Eucharistic Celebration," in *The Feast of Faith: Approaches to a Theology of Liturgy* (San Francisco: Ignatius, 1986), 33–60, at 51–60.

65. Dan. 3:17.

66. Dan. 3:11–12, 20.

67. Dan. 3:25 (3:92 New American Bible [NAB]).

68. Dan. 3:28 (3:95 NAB).

69. *Letter* 58.

70. "... if I deliver my body to be burned..." 1 Cor. 13:3.

71. *Letter* 173. Emphasis added.

72. Dan. 3:16–18, 20.

73. *Jacob and the Happy Life.*

74. See Cyprian, *Exhortation on Martyrdom Addressed to Fortunatus*, 11. The story of the Maccabeean martyrs is read in the liturgy for the Thirty-second Sunday in Ordinary Time (Year C) and on Tuesday and Wednesday of the Thirty-third Week in Ordinary Time (Year 1).

75. See William H. Brownlee, "From Holy War to Holy Martyrdom," in *Quest for the Kingdom*, eds. H. B. Huffman, F. A. Spina, A. R. W. Green (Winona Lake, IN: Eisenbrauns, 1983), 281–292.

76. 2 Macc. 6:3.

77. 2 Macc. 6:9–11.

78. See 2 Macc. 6:20, 31; 7:10, 20.

79. See 2 Macc. 7:22–23.

80. 2 Macc. 7:2.

81. 2 Macc. 6:28.

82. See 2 Macc. 6:30; 7:9, 11, 14, 23, 29.

83. 2 Macc. 7:17.

84. 2 Macc. 7:39.

Chapter 5: Be Not Afraid

1. *Gift and Mystery: On the Fiftieth Anniversary of My Priestly Ordination* (New York: Doubleday, 1996), 39.

2. General Audience (November 15, 1978).

3. *Crossing the Threshold of Hope* (New York: Alfred A. Knopf , 1994), 219.

4. Luke 1:30 (Greek: *mē phobou*). See also Luke 1:13.

5. Luke 5:10; John 6:20; Matt. 28:5, 10 (Greek: *mē phobeisthe*). See also Rev. 1:17 (Greek: *mē phobou*).

6. See for example, Gen. 15:1; Dan. 10:12, 19.

7. *The Four Cardinal Virtues*, 117.

8. *The Four Cardinal Virtues*, 134.

9. Luke 12:24; John 12:25.

10. Matt. 10:28; Luke 12:4.

11. *On the Morals of the Catholic Church*, chap. 22, 40.

12. Wisd. 2:23–24.

13. Rom. 5:12.

14. Eccles. 3:19.

15. Quoted in *Luke*, ed. Arthur A. Just, Jr., Ancient Christian Commentary on Scripture, New Testament 3 (Downers Grove, IL: InterVarsity, 2003), 18.

16. Heb. 2:14–15.

17. See Gen. 2:7; Ps. 90:3–6.

18. See Rom. 5:6; 6:17, 20; John 8:34.

19. 1 Cor. 15:32.

20. Sir. 40:1–5.

21. 1 John 3:8; compare John 12:31.

22. See 2 Tim. 1:10; 1 Cor. 15:26; Rev. 20:6.

23. Matt. 12:29; Mark 3:27; compare Isa. 49:24–26.

24. 1 Cor. 1:18 (Greek: *dynamis Theou*); see also Rom. 1:16.

25. 2 Cor. 13:4; compare Rom. 6:9–10.

26. Matt. 26:64 (Greek: *tēs Dynameōs*); Mark 14:62.

27. Col. 1:15–16.

28. Mark 4:41.

29. Isa. 9:6; 11:2–3.

30. Acts 10:38; compare Rom. 1:4; Luke 3:22; 4:1, 14.

31. See Luke 22:69; Rev. 12:10; Josh. 4:24; Wis. 7:25.

32. Luke 6:19 (Greek: *dynamis par autou exērcheto*); compare Mark 5:30.

33. Luke 24:49 (*ex hypsous dynamin*); see also Acts 1:8; 2:1–4.

34. Luke 10:19; compare Luke 9:1.

35. See for example, Acts 6:8.

36. *On the Incarnation of the Lord against Nestorius*, bk. 7, chap. 19.

37. Acts 3:12; compare 4:7, 10.

38. Rom. 15:18–19; compare 1 Cor. 2:2–5; 2 Cor. 6:7.

39. *Catechism*, no. 611.

40. *Theology of the Priesthood* (San Francisco: Ignatius, 1984), 73. The Greek word for "make" in all these verses is *"poiēsen,"* as we noted in the previous chapter.

41. Joseph Cardinal Ratzinger, *A New Song for the Lord: Faith in Christ and Liturgy Today* (New York: Crossroad, 1997), 175.

42. For this "minimalist" interpretation, which has proven to be very influential, see Raymond E. Brown, *Priest and Bishop: Biblical Reflections* (New York: Paulist, 1970).

43. Rom. 15:15–16.

44. For background on the language used here, see Joseph A. Fitzmyer, *Romans: A New Translation with Introduction and Commentary,* The Anchor Bible 33 (New York: Doubleday, 1992), 711–712. Compare Exod. 28:35, 43; 29:30.

45. Homily, Holy Mass for the Imposition of the Pallium on Metropolitan Archbishops on the Solemnity of the Holy Apostles Peter and Paul (June 29, 2008). See also Joseph Cardinal Ratzinger, "Eucharist and Mission," in *Pilgrim Fellowship of Faith*, 90–122, at 119.

46. 2 Cor. 5:20; Philem. 9.

47. Gal. 4:14.

48. 2 Cor. 2:10.

49. See Heb. 7:12; Eph. 5:2.

50. 2 Tim. 1:6.

51. Acts 9:12, 17; 13:2–3; 19:6–7; 1 Tim. 4:14

52. "Rite of Ordination of a Priest," 154, 156, in *Rites of Ordination of a Bishop, of Priests, and of Deacons*, 2nd Typical Ed. Washington, DC: U.S. Conference of Catholic Bishops, 2003).

53. Matt. 16:18.

54. 1 Cor. 15:26.

55. Acts 26:18; compare Luke 10:18.

56. Luke 10:17–19.

57. 2 Tim. 1:6–7.

58. Compare Heb. 13:9; Rom. 1:11; 16:25.

59. Eph. 3:16, 20.

60. Col. 1:11.

61. 1 Pet. 5:10.

62. *Christ in His Mysteries*, 8th ed. (St. Louis: B. Herder, 1939), 333.

63. See 1 Cor. 11:23–28; Acts 5:41.

64. Phil. 4:13.

65. 2 Cor. 11:23–28.

66. See John 10:25; 14:12.

67. 1 Cor. 1:18, 23–24.

68. See 1 Cor. 1:23, 25.

69. 1 Cor. 1:18.

70. Heb. 5:2; 4:15.

71. *Reasons for the Faith against Muslim Objections*, 7.

72. See Cardinal Joseph Ratzinger, "God's Power — Our Hope," in *A New Song for the Lord*, 37–55.

73. Compare Phil. 2:5–11.

74. Compare John 4:34; 5:30; compare John 10:17–18.

75. Matt. 26:39, 42, 44; compare Matt. 6:7.

76. Quoted in Ratzinger, *A New Song for the Lord*, 42.

77. *Epistle to the Philadelphians*, 7, 2. See also Wilken, *The Spirit of Early Christian Thought*, 264.

78. 1 Cor. 11:1; see also Eph. 5:1; 1 Thess. 1:6.

79. John 13:15.

80. John 10:11–16.

81. "What Do You Expect of a Priest?" in *Letters on Art and Literature* (New York: Philosophical Library, 1953), 17–28, at 22.

82. Second Vatican Council, *Optatum Totius*, 8.

83. *Reasons for the Faith against Muslim Objections*, 7.

84. *Tractates on the Gospel of John*, tr. 123, 5. Compare Vatican Congregation for the Clergy, *The Priest and the Third Christian Millennium: Teacher of the Word, Minister of the Sacraments, and Leader of the Community* (March 19, 1999), 32.

85. *Catechism*, no. 1589.

86. Quoted in *Colossians, 1–2 Thessalonians, 1–2 Timothy, Titus, Philemon*, ed. Peter Gorday, Ancient Christian Commentary on Scripture, New Testament 9 (Downers Grove, IL: InterVarsity, 2003), 232.

87. John 15:13.

88. 1 Cor. 16:13 (Greek: *andrizomai*).

89. See 1 Cor. 13:3.

90. Tit. 1:2.

91. Luke 20:27–39. On Jewish belief in the resurrection, see generally, Jon D. Levenson, *Resurrection and the Restoration of Israel: The Ultimate Victory of the God of Life* (New Haven: Yale University, 2008).

92. Compare Luke 16:30–31.

93. 1 Cor. 15:12–27.

94. Heb. 12:2.

95. 2 Cor. 13:4.

96. 2 Cor. 12:9–10.

97. Rev. 1:18.

98. General Audience (November 15, 1978).

99. See Mark 5:36; Matt. 24:13; John 16:33.

Chapter 6: The Image of God and the Perfection of Virtue

1. *The Silence of St. Thomas* (New York: Pantheon, 1957), 19.

2. *Summa Contra Gentiles*, bk. 1, chap. 2.

3. "St. Thomas, Servant of the Truth," in *Faith and the Spiritual Life* (New York: Herder and Herder, 1968), 67–85, at 68.

4. *The Dumb Ox* (New York: Image, 1956), 161–162.

5. See Rebecca Konyndyk De Young, "Power Made Perfect in Weakness: Aquinas's Transformation of the Virtue of Courage," *Medieval Philosophy and Theology* 11 (2003): 147–180, at 147–148.

6. Gen. 1:26.

7. International Theological Commission, *Communion and Stewardship: Human Persons Created in the Image of God* (2002), 16. Text published on-line at: http://www.vatican.va/roman_curia/congregations/cfaith/cti_documents/rc_con_cfaith_doc_20040723_communion-stewardship_en.html.

8. For Thomas's discussion of the *imago Dei*, see chiefly, *Summa Theologiae*, pt. 1a, q. 93. Hereafter cited *Summa*.

9. *Summa*, pt. 1a, q. 93, art. 4.

10. Compare Col. 1:15; 2 Cor. 4:4.

11. Compare Phil. 2:7.

12. *Catechism*, no. 1877. My reading of Thomas here and elsewhere is indebted to the fine work of Dominican Archbishop J. Augustine Di Noia and Domican Father Romanus Cessario. See Di Noia, "*Imago Dei–Imago Christi*: The Theological Foundations of Christian Humanism," *Nova et Vetera* 2:2 (Fall 2004): 267–279; Cessario, "Sonship, Sacrifice, and Satisfaction: The Divine Friendship in Aquinas and the Renewal of Christian Anthropology," *Letter & Spirit* 3 (2007): 71–93; see also Michael A. Dauphinais, "Loving the Lord Your God: The *Imago Dei* in St. Thomas Aquinas," *The Thomist* 63 (1999): 241–67.

13. *Catechism*, no. 1877.

14. *Summa Contra Gentiles*, bk. 3, 19.

15. *Summa*, pt. 1a–2ae, prol.

16. *omne agensagit propter finem; Summa Contra Gentiles*, bk. 3, chap. 2.

17. *Summa*, pt. 1a, q. 22, art. 2. Thomas is here citing the Latin Vulgate translation of Scripture.

18. *Summa*, pt. 1a–2ae, q. 65, art. 5.

19. *Summa*, pt. 1a, q. 77, art. 2.

20. *Summa*, pt. 1a-2ae, q. 5, art. 8.

21. *The Scope of the Summa* (Washington, DC: Thomist, 1958), 36; see also Stephen J. Pope, "Overview of the Ethics of Thomas Aquinas," in *The Ethics of Aquinas*, ed. Stephen J. Pope (Washington, DC: Georgetown University, 2002), 30–53, at 33.

22. *Summa*, pt. 1a–2ae, q. 5, art. 6.

23. *Summa*, pt. 1a, q. 78, art. 2.

24. *Summa*, pt. 1a, q. 78, art. 3–4.

25. *Summa*, pt. 1a, q. 79.

26. *Summa*, pt. 1a, q. 80–83.

27. *Summa*, pt. 2a–2ae, q. 2, art. 2; pt. 2a–2ae, q. 4, art. 2.

28. *Summa*, pt. 2a–2ae, q. 3, art. 2.

29. *Summa*, pt. 1a, q. 79, art. 13.

30. *Summa*, pt. 1a–2ae, q. 19, art. 5.

31. *Summa*, pt. 1a, q. 81, art. 1.

32. *Summa*, pt. 1a, q. 82, art. 5.

33. *Summa*, pt. 1a, art. 1, reply obj. 2.

34. *Summa*, pt. 1a, art. 2.

35. *Summa*, pt. 2a–2ae, q. 24, art. 3, reply obj. 3.

36. See the helpful discussion in Cessario, *The Virtues, or the Examined Life*, 158–159.

37. *Summa*, pt. 1a–2ae, q. 23, art. 1; compare art. 4.

38. Cessario, *The Virtues, or the Examined Life*, 160.

39. Rom. 7:15, 18.

40. *Summa*, pt. 1a–2ae, q. 56, art. 4, reply obj. 3. Emphasis added.

41. *Summa*, pt. 1a–2ae, q. 2, art. 8.

42. *Summa*, pt. 1a–2ae, q. 62, art. 1.

43. *Summa*, pt. 1a–2ae, q. 65, art. 2.

44. *Summa*, pt. 1a–2ae, q. 55, art. 1; cf. 1a–2ae, q. 56, a. 2. See John A. Oesterle's helpful introduction to his translation of Thomas's *Treatise on the Virtues* (Notre Dame, 1984), xiii.

45. *Summa*, pt. 1a–2ae, q. 49, art. 4.

46. *The Moral Virtues and Theological Ethics* (Notre Dame, IN: University of Notre Dame, 1991), 36.

47. Pinckaers, *The Sources of Christian Ethics*, 227.

48. *Summa*, pt. 2a–2ae, q. 123, art. 1. My translation, rather free at several points, is intended to illuminate Thomas's insights for pastoral care and development. Here I have benefited from the translation and discussion in William May's *An Introduction to Moral Theology*, 2nd. ed. (Huntington, IN: Our Sunday Visitor, 2003), 55–56.

49. *Summa*, pt. 1a–2ae, q. 61, art. 5. Translation from Oesterle, *Treatise on the Virtues*, 116.

50. *Summa*, pt. 1a–2ae, q. 61, art. 5. Translation from Oesterle, *Treatise on the Virtues*, 116.

51. *Summa*, pt. 1a–2ae, q. 62, art. 1.

52. *Summa*, pt. 1a–2ae, q. 63. See the excellent discussion of the "infused" virtues in Cessario, *The Moral Virtues and Theological Ethics*, 102–125.

53. *Summa*, pt. 1a–2ae, pt. 63, q. 3–4.

54. See T. C. O'Brien, "Virtue," in *New Catholic Encyclopedia*, 17 vols. (New York: McGraw-Hill), 15:704–708, at 706–708.

55. *Commentary on the Sentences*, bk. 3, dist. 33, q. 1, quoted in Cessario, *The Moral Virtues and Theological Ethics*, 110.

56. *Quaestio disputata de virtutibus in communi*, art. 10–11; in *Disputed Questions on Virtue*, trans. Ralph McInerny (South Bend, IN: St. Augustine's, 1999); see also *Summa*, pt. 1a–2ae, q. 110, art. 2.

57. *The Sources of Christian Ethics*, 180.

58. *Catechism*, nos. 1810–1811.

59. *Summa*, pt. 1a–2ae, q. 110, art. 3.

60. Cessario, *The Moral Virtues and Theological Ethics*, 112.

61. *The Moral Virtues and Theological Ethics*, 106.

62. *Summa*, pt. 3a, q. 7, art. 2.

63. *Summa*, pt. 1a–2ae, q. 110, art. 4.

64. *Summa*, pt. 1a–2ae, q. 61, art. 5.

65. Compare Rom. 8:29.

66. *The Primacy of Love: An Introduction to the Ethics of Thomas Aquinas* (New York: Paulist, 1992), 137–138.

67. *Summa*, pt. 1a–2ae, q. 68, art. 8.

68. *The Moral Virtues and Theological Ethics*, 52.

69. Pinckaers, *The Sources of Christian Ethics*, 178–179.

Chapter 7: Power Made Perfect in Weakness

1. *Apology*, 50 (Latin: *semen est sanguis christianorum*).

2. *Apology*, 50 (Latin: *vicimus cum occidimur*).

3. See Rev. 6:9; 19:13; 20:4.

4. Quoted in Eusebius, *The History of the Church*, bk. 5, chap. 2; compare Rev. 1:5; 3:14; Acts 3:15.

5. See Matt. 10:24–25; John 12:24.

6. *Ad Catholici Sacerdotii*, 7, 30.

7. See "The Narrative of the Expedition of Coronado, by Pedro de Castañeda," in *Spanish Explorers in the Southern United States, 1528–1543*, eds. Frederick W. Hodge and Theodore H. Lewis (Austin: Texas State Historical Association, 1990 [1907]), 364–365; 372–374.

8. Father Albert J. Nevins, M.M., *Our American Catholic Heritage* (Huntington, IN: Our Sunday Visitor, 1972), 48–49.

9. Quoted in Ann Ball, *Blessed Miguel Pro: A 20th-Century Mexican Martyr* (Rockford, IL: TAN, 1996), 67.

10. "Power Made Perfect in Weakness: Aquinas's Transformation of the Virtue of Courage," 150.

11. *Summa Theologiae*, pt. 2a–2ae, q. 124, art. 3.

12. *To the Romans*, 5–6.

13. Di Noia, "*Imago Dei–Imago Christi*," 274, 276–277. See also D. Juvenal Merriell, *To the Image of the Trinity: A Study in the Development of Aquinas's Teaching* (Toronto: Pontifical Institute of Medieval Studies, 1990); Ian A. McFarland, "When Time Is of the Essence: Aquinas and the *Imago Dei*," *New Blackfriars* 82 (2001): 208–223.

14. *The Virtues, or the Examined Life*, 167, n. 26; see also M.J. Congar, "Le Traité de la force dans la 'Somme théologique' de S. Thomas d'Aquin," *Angelicum* 51 (1974): 331–348.

15. *Summa*, pt. 3a, q. 1, art. 2; pt. 3a, q. 49, art. 4. See also the excellent article by Dominican Father Colman E. O'Neill, "The Priesthood of Christ (3a. 22)," in St. Thomas Aquinas, *Summa Theologiae*, vol. 50: The One Mediator (3a. 16–26) (London: Blackfriars, 1965), 245–249.

16. *Summa*, pt. 3a, q. 22, art. 1. Thomas cites Mal. 2:7 and Heb. 5:1.

17. *Summa*, pt. 3a, q. 22, art. 1.

18. "The Idea of the Church in St. Thomas Aquinas," in *The Mystery of the Church* (Baltimore: Helicon, 1960), 97–117, at 115.

19. *Summa*, pt. 3a, q. 62, art. 5; compare Eph. 5:2.

20. *Summa*, pt. 3a, q. 62, art. 5; compare John 19:34.

21. *Summa*, pt. 3a., q. 63, art. 3.

22. *Summa*, pt. 3a, q. 62, art. 5; compare John 19:34.

23. *Summa*, pt. 3a, q. 63, art. 3.

24. *Summa*, pt. 3a, q. 61, art. 1, reply obj. 3; pt. 3a, q. 84, art. 5, reply obj. 2.

25. *Summa*, pt. 3a, q. 61, art. 3.

26. *Summa*, pt. 3a, q. 62, art. 2.

27. *Summa*, suppl., q. 17, art. 2, reply obj. 5.

28. *Summa*, pt. 3a, q. 62, art. 1.

29. *Summa*, pt. 3a, q. 63, art. 1l; compare pt. 3a, q. 22, art. 1.

30. *Summa*, pt. 3a, q. 82, art. 3.

31. *Summa*, pt. 3a., q. 22, art. 4.

32. *Summa*, suppl., q. 34, art. 2.

33. *Summa*, pt. 3a, q. 63, art. 4, 6.

34. *Summa*, pt. 3a, q. 34, art. 2.

35. *Summa*, suppl., q. 34, art. 1, contra.

36. *Summa*, suppl., q. 34, art. 1.

37. *Summa*, pt. 3a, q. 73, art. 3.

38. *Summa*, suppl., q. 37, art. 2, reply obj. 3.

39. *Summa*, suppl., q. 40, art. 4.

40. *Summa*, suppl., q. 17, art. 1.

41. *Summa*, pt. 3a, q. 1. 79, art. 1; suppl., q. 34, art. 1, reply obj. 3.

42. *Summa*, pt. 3a, q. 63, art. 2.

43. *Summa*, pt. 3a, q. 84, art. 4, reply obj. 3; compare *Summa*, suppl., q. 34, art. 1.

44. *Summa*, pt. 3a, q. 63, art. 3.

45. *Summa*, pt. 3a, q. 63, art. 6.

46. *Summa*, pt. 3a, q. 82, art. 1.

47. *Summa*, pt. 3a, q. 82, art. 5.

48. *Summa*, pt. 3a, q. 83, art. 1, reply obj. 3.

49. *Summa*, pt. 3a., q. 84, art. 1.

50. *Summa*, pt. 3a., q. 84, art 3, reply obj. 3.

51. *Summa*, pt. 3a., q. 78, art. 1.

52. *Summa*, pt. 3, q. 37, art. 1, obj. 2. Thomas cites here Pope Innocent III's *Sermon* 22. On this aspect of Thomas's teaching, see Richard

Schenk, "*Omnis Christi actio nostra est instructio:* The Deeds and Sayings of Jesus as Revelation in the View of Thomas Aquinas," in *Studi Tomistici* 37 (Vatican City: Libreria Editrice, 1990); Michael J. Dodds, "The Teaching of Thomas Aquinas on the Mysteries of the Life of Christ," in *Aquinas on Doctrine: A Critical Introduction,* eds. Thomas Weinandy, Daniel Keating, and John Yocum (London: T&T Clark, 2004), 91–116.

53. *Summa,* pt. 3a, prol.

54. "The Idea of the Church in St. Thomas Aquinas," 108. See also Thomas Hibbs, "*Imitatio Christi* and the Foundation of Aquinas's Ethics," *Communio* 18 (1991): 556–73.

55. *De rationibus fidei contra Saracenos, Graecos et Armenos ad Cantorem Antiochenum,* chap. 7; in *Aquinas: On Reasons for Our Faith Against the Muslims, and a Reply to the Denial of Purgatory by Certain Greeks and Armenians, to the Cantor of Antioch,* ed. James Likoudis (New Bedord, MA: Franciscans of the Immaculate, 2002).

56. *Compendium Theologiae* [The Compendium of Theology], 201; in *Light of Faith: The Compendium of Theology* (Manchester, NH: Sophia Institute, 1993), 230; see also *Collationes super Credo in Deum* [Explanations of the Creed], 6. Text in *The Three Greatest Prayers: Commentaries on the Lord's Prayer, the Hail Mary, and the Apostles' Creed* (Manchester, NH: Sophia Institute, 1990), 51.

57. *De rationibus fidei,* chap. 7.

58. *Lectura super Johannem,* chap. 1, lect. 8, 189–190. Text in *Commentary on the Gospel of John,* trans. James A. Weisheiphl and Fabian R. Larcher, Aquinas Scripture Series 4 (Albany, NY: Magi, 1980).

59. *Lectura super Johannem,* chap. 1, lect. 14, 260, 273.

60. See, for example, *Lectura super Johannem,* chap. 7, lect. 2, 1034; chap. 11, lect. 8, 1584.

61. *Collationes super Credo in Deum,* 4.

62. *Commentary on the Epistle to the Hebrews,* 667; text in *Commentary on the Epistle to the Hebrews* (South Bend, IN: St. Augustine's Press, 2006); see also *Summa Theologiae,* pt. 3a, q. 46, art. 4; compare Augustine, *Tractates on John,* 119.

63. *Compendium Theologiae,* 227.

64. *Compendium Theologiae,* 227. Emphasis added.

65. *Lectura super Johannem,* chap. 1, lect. 8, 190; compare *Summa,* pt. 3a, q. 69, art. 4–7.

66. *Commentary on the Epistle to the Colossians,* 145; text in *Commentary on Colossians,* ed. and trans. Fabian R. Larcher and Daniel A. Keating (Naples, FL: Sapientia, 2006).

67. *Summa,* pt. 2a–2ae, q. 123, art. 2., obj. 2; reply obj. 2.

68. *Rise, Let Us Be on Our Way* (New York: Warner, 2004), 190.

69. See Taylor's essay, "A Catholic Modernity?" in *A Catholic Modernity? Charles Taylor's Marianist Award Lecture,* ed. James L. Heft (New York: Oxford University, 1999), 13–38.

70. 2 Tim. 4:2.

71. *Summa*, pt. 2a–2ae, q. 126–127.

72. *Summa*, pt. 2a–2ae. q. 123, art. 3.

73. *Summa*, pt. 2a–2ae, q. 123, art. 3.

74. *Summa*, pt. 2a–2ae, q. 123, art. 1 (Latin: *fortitudo mentis*).

75. *The Virtues, or the Examined Life*, 167.

76. *Summa*, pt. 2a–2ae, q. 123, art. 4.

77. For Aquinas's treatment of fear, see the *Summa*, pt. 1a–2ae, q. 41–43.

78. *Summa*, pt. 2a–2ae, q. 123, art. 3.

79. *Summa*, pt. 2a–2ae, q. 125, art. 2.

80. *Summa*, pt. 2a–2ae, q. 123, art. 4, reply obj. 2; compare Konyndyk De Young, "Power Made Perfect in Weakness," at 152.

81. *Summa*, pt. 2a–2ae, q. 125, art. 2.

82. Heb. 2:14–15.

83. *Compendium Theologiae*, 227.

84. *Summa*, pt. 2a–2ae, q. 123, art. 12.

85. *Summa*, pt. 2a–2ae, q. 129, art. 6; compare pt. 2a–2ae, q. 123, art. 2, reply obj. 2.

86. *Summa*, pt. 2a–2ae, q. 123, art. 5.

87. *Summa*, pt. 2a–2ae, q. 123, art. 5.

88. *Summa*, pt. 2a–2ae, q. 124, art. 3. Emphasis added.

89. *Summa*, pt. 2a–2ae, q. 123, art. 5.

90. *Summa*, pt. 2a–2a3, q. 124, art. 5, reply obj. 3.

91. General Audience (November 15, 1978); compare John Paul's *Veritatis Splendor*, Encyclical Letter Regarding Certain Fundamental Questions of the Church's Moral Teaching (August 6, 1998), 42.

92. *Catechism*, no. 1808.

93. "Power Made Perfect in Weakness," at 180.

94. Also quoted by Konyndyk De Young, "Power Made Perfect in Weakness," at 150, n. 13.

95. *On the Morals of the Catholic Church*, 15, quoted in *Summa*, pt. 2a–2ae, q. 123, art. 7, obj. 3.

96. *Commentary on the Epistle to the Colossians*, chap. 2, 89.

97. See, for example, *Lectura super Johannem*, chap. 2, lect. 1, 335; chap. 11, lect. 2, 1485; chap. 20, lect. 3, 2518, 2524; chap. 20, lect. 4, 2537.

98. *Commentary on the First Epistle to the Corinthians*, chap. 1, 18.

99. *Explanations of the Our Father*, in *Three Greatest Prayers*, 137.

100. *Summa*, pt. 2a–2ae, q. 123, art. 2, reply obj. 2.

101. *Summa*, pt. 2a–2ae, q. 129, art. 1.

102. *Summa*, pt. 2a–2ae, q. 134.

103. *Summa*, pt. 2a–2ae, q. 130, art. 1, reply obj. 3.

104. *Summa*, pt. 2a–2ae, q. 131, art. 1.

105. See generally, Father Basil Cole, O.P., *The Hidden Enemies of the Priesthood: The Contributions of St. Thomas Aquinas* (Staten Island, NY:

Alba House, 2007), esp. chap. 7: "Vainglory: The Problems of Praise in the Priesthood."

106. *Summa*, pt. 2a–2ae, q. 133.

107. *Summa*, pt. 2a–2ae, q. 135.

108. *Summa*, pt. 2a–2ae, q. 136.

109. *Summa*, pt. 2a–2ae, q. 137.

110. *Catechism*, nos. 1266, 1299, 1830.

111. *Summa*, pt. 2a–2ae, q. 139, art. 1; see also Pope John Paul II, *Letter to Priests for Holy Thursday 1998*, 3–5.

112. *Summa*, pt. 1a–2ae, q. 63, art. 3.

113. *The Mystical Evolution*, 1:212–213.

114. *Commentary on the Epistle to the Hebrews*, chap. 2, 144–147.

115. "Fortitude," in St. Thomas Aquinas, *Summa Theologiae*, First Complete American Edition, vol. 3 (New York: Benzinger Brothers, 1948), 3393–3400, at 3399.

116. *Commentary on the Epistle to the Hebrews*, chap. 2, 144–147.

117. *Quodlibetal Questions* 5, q. 3, art. 2; in *Meditations for Lent from St. Thomas Aquinas*, trans. Father Philip Hughes (Fort Collins, CO: Roman Catholic Books, n.d.), 121–122.

Chapter 8: His Heart Was Courageous in the Ways of the Lord

1. *The Sanctifier* (Paterson, NJ: St. Anthony Guild, 1957), 136.

2. Rom. 1:7; 1 Cor. 1:2.

3. 1 Cor. 15:42; compare Matt. 13:31; John 12:24.

4. *On the Mysteries*, chap. 7, 39.

5. Quoted in *The Essential Pope Benedict XVI*, 316.

6. Quoted in Vincent J. O'Malley, C. M., *Saints of North America* (Huntington, IN: Our Sunday Visitor, 2004), 61.

7. See *The Kolbe Reader: The Writings of St. Maximilian M. Kolbe, O.F.M. Cov.*, ed. Anselm W. Romb, O.F.M. Conv. (Libertyville, IL: Franciscan Marytown Press, 1987), 67.

8. Compare Song 8:6.

9. Quoted in Jacques Leclerq, *Man of God for Others* (Westminster, MD: Newman, 1968), 39.

10. Matt. 19:27. Compare Matt. 10:37–39; 19:27–30.

11. John 15:16.

12. 1 Cor. 4:1; 1 Pet. 4:10.

13. Address to Clergy at Warsaw Cathedral (May 25, 2006).

14. Address to Clergy at Warsaw Cathedral.

15. *Gift and Mystery*, 72–73; compare at 44: "Just as in Mass the Holy Spirit brings about the transubstantiation of the bread and wine into the Body and Blood of Christ, so also in the Sacrament of Holy Orders he effects the priestly or episcopal consecration."

16. *Summa Theologiae,* suppl., q. 40, art. 4.

17. See Joseph Cardinal Ratzinger, *Called to Communion: Understanding the Church* (San Francisco: Ignatius, 1996), 127–128.

18. Compare Col. 1:20.

19. *Catechism,* no. 1082; John Paul, *Gift and Mystery,* 74–75.

20. *Christ the Ideal of the Priest* (San Francisco: Ignatius, 2005 [1952]), 21.

21. Compare Gal. 1:6.

22. 2 Cor. 11:23–28.

23. Address to Clergy in Warsaw Cathedral.

24. *Of the Morals of the Catholic Church,* chap. 32, 69.

25. See 1 Pet. 5:8

26. *Pathways to Holiness,* trans. and adapt. by Jordan Aumann, O.P. (New York: Alba House, 1998), 82–83.

27. *Pathways to Holiness,* 83.

28. Compare 1 Cor. 1:18; Heb. 1:3; 2 Cor. 13:4; Rom. 6:9–10.

29. See Second Vatican Council, *Presbyterorum Ordinis,* 12–13.

30. *Spiritual Theology,* 229.

31. *Pastores Dabo Vobis,* 82.

32. *Christ the Ideal of the Priest,* 69.

33. "The Ministry and Life of Priests," in *The Essential Pope Benedict XVI,* 315.

34. Office of Readings (November 4), *Liturgy of the Hours,* 4:1545.

35. John 19:10.

36. *The Spiritual Life,* 516.

37. Compare John 6:44.

38. *Summa,* pt. 1a–2ae, q. 62, art. 1, reply obj. 3.

39. Rom. 7:15.

40. 1 Thess. 4:3.

41. Phil. 4:13.

42. *Letter* 10, 3.

43. Luke 18:14.

44. *Catechism,* no. 489; compare no. 273.

45. See Luke 1:46–55, 68–79.

46. Luke 1:73; compare 1 Cor. 15:26.

47. Compare 2 Cor. 5:17; Gal. 6:15.

48. *Catechism,* no. 1266; compare no. 1810.

49. Office of Readings (November 23), *Liturgy of the Hours,* 4:1581–1582.

50. *The Definition of Moral Virtue* (New York: Fordham University, 1986), 51.

51. *Moral Virtues and Theological Ethics,* 112.

52. *In the Redeeming Christ: Toward a Theology of Spirituality* (New York: Sheed & Ward, 1963), 141, 143.

53. Rom. 6:3–4.

54. "Priestly Celibacy: Sign of the Charity of Christ," available at http://www.vatican.va/roman_curia/congregations/cclergy/documents/rc_con_cclergy_doc_01011993_sign_en.html.

55. Matt. 7:7.

56. Luke 17:5.

57. Rom. 15:13.

58. Phil. 1:9.

59. *The Aquinas Prayer Book* (Manchester, NH: Sophia Institute, 2000), 33–35.

60. *Talks to Priests*, 48–49.

61. See Rosmini's chapter on "Meditation and the Divine Office," in *Talks to Priests*, 43–60; and Marmion, "The *Opus Dei*, Means of Union of God," in *Christ the Ideal of the Monk*, 5th ed. (St. Louis: B. Herder, 1926), 310–336; "The Divine Office," in *Christ the Ideal of the Priest*, 255–274.

62. Pius X, *Divino Afflatu*, in Office of Readings (August 21), *Liturgy of the Hours*, 4:1336.

63. *Christ the Ideal of the Monk*, 314.

64. Ps. 70:1.

65. *Homilies on the First Epistle of St. John*, Homily 7, 8.

66. Quoted in O'Malley, *Saints of North America*, 393–394.

67. *Treatise on the Love of God*, bk. 12, chap. 9 (Rockford, IL: TAN, 1997); compare Marmion, *Christ the Life of the Soul*, 231.

68. *Christ the Ideal of the Priest*, 156.

69. 1 Cor. 10:31; 11:1; compare John 4:34; 5:30; 6:38; 17:4.

70. *Sources of Christian Ethics*, 356; compare Tanquerey, *The Spiritual Life*, 509.

71. Aumann, *Spiritual Theology*, 314.

72. *Spiritual Theology*, 315.

73. On this idea of "offering up" our sufferings, see Pope Benedict XVI, *Spe Salvi*, Encyclical Letter on Christian Hope (November 30, 2007), 40.

74. Ps. 34:19.

75. Sir. 2:1–6.

76. John 16:33.

77. Acts 14:22.

78. 2 Tim. 3:12.

79. See Heb. 12:1–11; compare Prov. 3:11–12.

80. *Lectura super Johannem*, chap. 9, lect. 1, 1302.

81. *Lectura super Johannem*, chap. 15, lect. 1, 1985; compare John 15:2; See also Aquinas, *Commentary on the Second Epistle to the Corinthians*, 472.

82. Rom. 5:2–5.

83. 1 Pet. 2:21.

84. *The Spiritual Life*, 73.

85. *Christ Is Passing By: Homilies* (Chicago: Scepter, 1974), 149–150.

86. 1 Thess. 2:13.

87. *Christ, the Ideal of the Monk,* 318–319.

88. *The Rites of the Catholic Church as Revised by the Second Vatican Ecumenical Council,* 2 vols. (New York: Pueblo, 1979), 2:63; compare Marmion, *Christ the Ideal of the Priest,* 64.

89. Phil. 3:8–10.

90. John 15:15.

91. Compare 2 Cor. 12:9–10.

92. *The Pursuit of Happiness — God's Way: Living the Beatitudes* (New York: Alba House, 1998), 178–179.

93. *Sermon* 304; in Office of Readings (August 10), *Liturgy of the Hours* 4:1305–1306.

94. 1 Pet. 2:5.

95. See Phil. 2:17.

96. See Eph. 5:27; Phil. 2:15; 1 Tim. 2:3; 5:4; compare Col. 1:10; 2 Thess. 1:11.

97. Rom. 12:1–2; Heb. 13:15.

98. *Homily* 32 on the Gospels; quoted in Rosmini, *Talks to Priests,* 145.

99. *Commentary on the Second Epistle to the Corinthians,* 186.

100. Compare Prov. 31:10; 1 Cor. 1:24.

101. 2 Chron. 17:6.

About the Author

THE MOST REVEREND JOSÉ H. GOMEZ, S.T.D., is the Archbishop of San Antonio, Texas. He was installed as Archbishop in 2005. Prior to that, he served as Auxiliary Bishop of the Archdiocese of Denver, appointed a bishop by Pope John Paul II in 2001.

Born in 1951 in Monterrey, Mexico, Archbishop Gomez was ordained a priest of the Opus Dei Prelature in 1978. He holds a doctorate in Sacred Theology as well as degrees in philosophy and accounting. He is the author of *A Will to Live: Clear Answers on End of Life Issues* (Basilica, 2006) and two pastoral letters: *To Grow in Knowledge and Love of Jesus Christ* (2006) and *The Tender Mercy of Our God* (2007). In his many homilies, public talks, and writings, Archbishop Gomez stresses the need for a new evangelization of American culture and for Catholics to bear witness to their faith — in their homes, in their workplaces, and in their political lives.

Archbishop Gomez is an enthusiastic advocate of vocations to the priesthood and religious life. He played a key role in the establishment in 2000 of the Hispanic Seminary of Our Lady of Guadalupe in Mexico City, which educates Hispanic seminarians to serve in the United States. His own archdiocesan seminary, Assumption Seminary, is among the nation's leading institutions of priestly formation.

A leader in the nation's Hispanic community, Archbishop Gomez has served as the president of the National Association of Hispanic Priests and was instrumental in the founding of the Catholic Association of Latino Leaders. He has served as the founding chairman of the U.S. bishops' Committee on Cultural Diversity in the Church and serves on the U.S. bishops' Committee on Doctrine. In 2008, Pope Benedict XVI appointed him as a consultant to the Pontifical Commission for Latin America.

Notes

Notes

Notes

Notes

Notes

Notes